Praise for *Naylor's Natter*

'The *Naylor's Natter* book is a superb read of some of the best advice and tips from Phil's podcast, distilled into an easy-to-read and humorous account. The soundbites from guests and QR code links to the episodes serve as a wonderful and thorough guide through topics such as CPD, behaviour and leadership. I loved this!'
Rachel Ball, assistant principal teaching and learning, @MrsBallAP

'Phil's ability to identify the golden nuggets in each and every conversation makes this an invaluable read for every educator. A brilliant translation from podcast to book.'
Toria Bono, teacher and host of Tiny Voice Talks podcast, @Toriaclaire

'An inspiring read that distils hundreds of hours of the combined knowledge and experience of so many educationalists. Packed full of practical strategies and recommendations, this book offers plenty of opportunities to challenge your own thinking.'
Stacey Cantley, ECT lead

'Phil Naylor leads us on a brisk Cook's Tour of current educational thinking in England, distilling from his many online "natters" a range of blessedly non-partisan and down-to-earth nuggets of wisdom about how best to run a classroom and a school.'
Professor Guy Claxton, author of *The Future of Teaching and the Myths that Hold It Back*, @GuyClaxton

'Naylor's Natter has come a long way since the first episode, recorded many years ago in our school's sixth form library. This book does a fantastic job of transferring the podcast's accessible and friendly tone to print, and features pearls of wisdom from some true giants of teaching. Highly recommended!'
Simon Cox, Director of Blackpool Research School, @MathsMrCox

'A fascinating read with so many words of wisdom offered and takeaways for every teacher. The likeable, humble and enthusiastic Phil Naylor has brought those qualities and more to his book as well as shining a spotlight on some great individuals in education. A recommended read that has the potential to lead to further conversations and reflections in any school.'
Kate Jones, teacher and author, @KateJones_teach

'A marvellous account of the creation of a highly acclaimed podcast plus a distillation of the main things that make a difference. Great work!'
Mary Myatt, education writer and curator at Myatt & Co, @MaryMyatt

'I was unsure whether it is because I'm from the same era, socio-economic background or geographical area as Phil that I couldn't put this down, then I realised, it's just because it is great – easy to navigate, speaks from the heart and what we all need: simplicity and depth rolled into one.'
Lizy Oakes, assistant vice principal teaching and learning, @LizyOakes

'Packed full of educational wisdom, this book represents a range of voices from across the sector. It is wonderfully concise for real impact, with the bonus of links to the original podcasts to explore ideas further.'
Cat Rushton, assistant principal (teaching and learning), @CatherineRusht2

'This book is accessible and useful. A compendium that can be used for occasional reference or just as easily be read in one sitting. Logical chapters and ordering along with "Naylor's nuggets" and reflective exercises mean it will be one of those books you return to. Useful for teachers and school leaders alike.'
Professor Toby Salt, former CEO of Ormiston Academies Trust and AQA, author of *The Juggling Act*

'In a seamless segue from podcast to page, Phil Naylor has brought together the wit, wisdom and experience of multiple expert contributors in perfect harmony – with his trademark warmth, deep knowledge and passion for education.'
Emma Turner FCCT, Discovery Trust Research and CPD Lead, and author, @Emma_Turner75

Naylor's Natter

Ideas and advice from the collective wisdom of teachers, as heard on the popular education podcast

Phil Naylor

BLOOMSBURY EDUCATION

LONDON OXFORD NEW YORK NEW DELHI SYDNEY

BLOOMSBURY EDUCATION
Bloomsbury Publishing Plc
50 Bedford Square, London, WC1B 3DP, UK
29 Earlsfort Terrace, Dublin 2, Ireland

BLOOMSBURY, BLOOMSBURY EDUCATION and the Diana logo are trademarks of
Bloomsbury Publishing Plc

First published in Great Britain, 2022 by Bloomsbury Publishing Plc

This edition published in Great Britain, 2022 by Bloomsbury Publishing Plc

A catalogue record for this book is available from the British Library

ISBN: PB: 978-1-4729-9246-8; ePDF: 978-1-4729-9244-4; ePub: 978-1-4729-9245-1

2 4 6 8 10 9 7 5 3 1 (paperback)

Typeset by Newgen KnowledgeWorks Pvt. Ltd., Chennai, India
Printed and bound in the UK by CPI Group Ltd, CR0 4YY

To find out more about our authors and books visit www.bloomsbury.com and
sign up for our newsletters

Contents

Acknowledgements

I would firstly like to thank all the guests who have given freely of their time to educate me and our wonderful listeners. I must also thank Hannah Marston from Bloomsbury for believing that I had a book in me and for her eternal patience through what has been a very challenging first writing experience.

I would like to dedicate this book to my children Liam and Ayda-Rose with a large nod to my mother Sylvia, my father Bill and my siblings Anthony and Alison. I hope this gives them a source of some pride that a working-class lad from Wigan can 'knock out' an education book having enjoyed a fully comprehensive education in Accrington. If I can, anybody can.

I must also cite an underserved but not insignificant influence on my improved productivity. An influence in my life five years ago showed me that the road to success is paved with extremely hard work and dedication, much more than I had ever realised. Endeavours like this are not completed without effort levels that I saw first-hand and have influenced me ever since. For that and nothing else, I must thank them.

Phil Naylor
February 2022

Introduction: A rationale for podcast pedagogy

3rd January 2019, Naylor's Natter launches to rapturous reception from thousands of expectant teachers just waiting for a weekly dose of educational expertise dropping into their podcast provider of choice… well, not quite!

At the time of Naylor's Natter's inception, I was the self-titled Assistant Director of Blackpool Research School, part of the Research Schools Network, a collaboration between the Institute for Effective Education (IEE) and the Education Endowment Foundation (EEF). (I'd seen the title 'Director' on future guest Alex Quigley's door at Huntington School and decided to adopt my title.) Future guests Stephen Tierney, Simon Cox and I were looking at ways to promote our upcoming researchED Blackpool conference. The prevailing wisdom amongst us at the time was to explore Stephen's book of Twitter contacts and persuade them to appear by offering them a night in Blackpool. This approach had begun to work; we had a stellar list of speakers and a venue that could hold 600 guests. As the weeks rolled by the tickets sold gradually, but we were struggling to get the required interest in the conference to justify our venue choice. We looked at paid marketing, promoted tweets, sponsored Facebook posts and all manner of networking, but nothing really captured the zeitgeist.

At one of our regular meetings with Stephen, I tentatively floated the idea of a Blackpool Research School podcast. This was far from a new idea and one that I had clearly plagiarised from the guru of podcasting, namely Mr Craig Barton. This idea met with a positive response from both Stephen and Simon but with one sticking point:

> 'Probably best not to call it the Blackpool Research School podcast. We don't want to damage the brand if it isn't very good.'

A very sage point at the time as the research movement was in its infancy and the Research Schools had to ensure they were on message. As someone without a brand to tarnish, I happily volunteered to put my name to the podcast and take any brickbats that may come my way. Note that it is 'Naylor's Natter', singular, meaning I only ever expected there to be one episode.

Looking back from the vantage point of a pandemic-scarred 2022, it is easy to forget that buried deep inside computers in 2019 we had all the technology required to easily record, edit and distribute a podcast. But I either didn't know or didn't look because the earliest episode features Simon Cox and me recorded live into an iPad and then emailed across straight to anchor. As you would expect, the episode sunk without much of a trace (despite Simon's excellent interview – use the QR code on page 23 to have a listen). As it went largely unnoticed, this provided breathing space to at least begin to hone the craft of interviewing, source guests from Stephen's contacts and invest in some sound effects and jingles.

Ah, the jingle... You're singing it now, aren't you? I'd love to claim credit for its earworm status and of course I do retain writing credits for the lyrics at least. This came about through friend of the show Benjamin D. Barker, who was already an established host, recommending a website called Fiverr which allowed creators to advertise their craft to budding entrepreneurs. I figured to sound more professional, Naylor's Natter would need some voice overs and jingles. I invested in numerous versions, some you can still hear in early episodes, but one really stood out. The jingle that has adorned most of our output since then was recorded by an established American country artist who, like me, was just dipping his toe into the new technology. This was without doubt the best £17 I have ever spent. He must be aware of the podcast's prominence now as I asked him for a new version recently, but the price had increased exponentially!

With a jingle in place, we then needed to up our game with guests, and a notable early coup was Professor Daniel Muijs (at the time Ofsted's Head of Research). The excitement in the Research School broom cupboard when he was confirmed was palpable. Whilst our marketing had progressed, our sound had not. For any reader expecting George Martin sitting behind a mixing desk whilst Simon and I stroked our beards, chewing the research fat with Ofsted's head honcho, think again. This episode was Simon and me with a hastily arranged 'Do not disturb' sticky note on the research cupboard door on the phone to Daniel with the voice recorder from an iPad trying to pick up the sound! We got away with that one as the small room enhanced the audio; I was not so lucky when I lured one of education's titans Professor Michael Young onto the show. Michael was a delight to host, and I remain a huge admirer of his work, but the audio was so bad it is almost unplayable. These episodes increased our listener base significantly, our ticket sales modestly and our negative reviews judiciously.

I am a firm believer in the positive power of social media. The support received for this book has kept me going through its 18-month gestation. In the early days of the podcast, we had some great support. An early supporter and one whose influence can still be heard was Ollie Lovell. Ollie is an extremely successful and respected podcaster in his own right, and I wholeheartedly recommend his ERRR podcast to all readers. In the early months of 2019, he got in touch with me to ask what software I used for recording the podcast. Somewhat taken aback, I replied that I used a phone, an iPad and an anchor! He was so generous in his advice around selecting a microphone, using GarageBand and Audacity, and how to improve our production. This advice made a huge difference, and his generosity is something I have tried to emulate with new podcasters to welcome them into our thriving community.

We started to settle on a formula which has seen some iterations, but the core concepts have remained the same. I personally enjoy many different kinds of interview, whether this be education, politics, history or sport. Where I do take issue and usually turn over is when an interview becomes more about the interviewer than the interviewee. When I was discussing my interviewing style in the early days, I rather impertinently compared myself (in style – not quality) to the great Michael Parkinson. I would like to ask prepared questions to allow the guest to feel comfortable, I would read everything I reasonably could about their work to be informed and I would never interrupt. I would of course allow some natural follow-up but never at the expense of the guest's contribution. I think at the time, and even now, this marks Naylor's Natter out as different from other podcasts and is the reason we have expanded across the world.

The formula became about continued professional development (CPD) for me as the host and then hopefully vicariously for the listener. If I was gaining professionally by having one-to-one access to these experts, then surely the listener would also be benefitting from their wisdom. My vision became and remained that if one person benefits from the conversation then it is worth doing. I have often been reminded of the power of this when I return from work, exhausted and caught up in the thick of thin things, and I have a podcast scheduled at 7pm meaning I literally have 23 minutes to get ready! As I slump into my recording chair, I summon up enough energy to get started. But when the podcast starts and the knowledge of the guests and their enthusiasm for their subject infuse me with a new energy, I imagine listeners having the same feeling. I hope they bound into school the following day imbued with new ideas that they can share. This is our *raison d'être*.

The podcast succeeded in attracting our guests with some notable education figures gracing early episodes. Once you had interviewed Person X, it made it much easier to interview Person Y and this culminated for me with the episode where I interviewed E. D. Hirsch. Having seen at first hand the influence of Don's work through involvement in the research and evidence movement, I literally had to pinch myself when he agreed through his PA to appear. My preparation, always thorough, hit new levels in anticipation of a conference with the great man. The day itself was everything I expected and more. I can still recall the Skype dialling tone fading as the camera switched on to Hirsch resplendent on a leather armchair in a palatial office in America. The titan of knowledge must have wondered what he had signed up for as he gazed upon a young Ken Bruce, sat on a computer desk amongst Minnie Mouse teddies in child number two's bedroom! These conversations hopefully serve to inform and inspire the reader that anyone can become involved in podcasting and further their own professional growth on the way.

Collaboration has been a huge part of the show over the years. The first supporters of the podcast, with time, resources, equipment and moral support were the Teacher Development Trust (TDT). I cannot express my gratitude enough to David Weston and the team, who as well as buying me my first 'proper' microphone contributed influential sections to many of the first 100 episodes. TDT were able to connect us to many of the guests we interviewed; they were also able to have their collective finger on the educational pulse, often guiding the listener to the latest research, evidence and CPD. TDT decided to go their own way in 2020, but they have remained supporters of the podcast. A public thanks is due to them all and I wouldn't be in a position to write a book without them. As 2020 began and the pandemic hit, it allowed time for reflection. I felt that seeing the world as I did through the paradigm of secondary education and a senior leader of some ten years' standing wasn't the only vista that the listeners needed. I felt that it was important for our listeners to diversify both our topics and our presenters. Many teachers have helped to co-host and indeed host Naylor's Natter over the last three years and each of them has brought a unique perspective. This is a feature that we intend to continue.

Features have been, well, a feature of Naylor's Natter since the beginning and something that my restless energy has been channelled into with a varying degree of success. As lockdown hit in early 2020, I started a book and film review section. The thinking was that the short three-week lockdown could give teachers an opportunity to delve into areas that previously their busy lives had prohibited. I'd long been a fan of *Kermode and Mayo's Film Review* on BBC Radio 5 Live and attempted to channel my inner critic to signpost listeners to classic films. The feedback was non-existent, and this feature slowly ebbed away and has never been reprised. The book reviews have had much more success and have now become the staple of the show. Thanks to the explosion in teacher authors and books about education, I decided to look into reviewing them. This was slightly at odds with my non-judgemental approach to the podcast and therefore precluded some books that I was either not interested by or some that I intrinsically avoided.

The Vinyl Suite is another feature that has proved to be very popular indeed but hugely time-consuming. The concept came from the office Andrew Perman and I shared at school at the time. Being two gentlemen of a certain age, confirmed audiophiles and music snobs, we decided that a record player was the perfect addition to our office. The thinking was to ease our path through the pastoral trials and tribulations of a Blackpool day and help to educate the young people and the teachers about the importance of music. The selections opened up discussions that were outside of the normal conversations in schools, which so often start:

'Did you get my email?' Any colleague, every school

The format is an education version of *Desert Island Discs* where listeners get to see behind the curtain and into the lives of our guests. Some of the suggestions have made a huge contribution to the making of this book. The two best exponents of the art of the Vinyl Suite were Dave McPartlin and Doug Lemov. Their episodes, featuring stories behind their choices, continue to attract large audiences months after their release. Dave shared his and Flakefleet's journey to the *Britain's Got Talent* final and their bid for Christmas number one. His choice of Dire Straits' *Local Hero* and Queen's *Don't Stop Me Now* raised the hairs on the back of my neck and really emphasised the power of music to shape people's lives. Doug Lemov, unscripted, hit upon a golden formula for the Vinyl Suite where he shared what he was listening to as he wrote his epic *Teach Like a Champion 3.0* (2021). Doug challenged the listener to see if they could hear the music coming through the pages of the book and with it opened up listeners' collections to music that they may not have ordinarily sought out. I have bought, shared and treasured many records as a result of this feature and at the time of writing I am listening to William Basinski – thank you, Simon Cox.

Having begun to diversify the range of guests and the presenters on the podcast, I had become open to voices all across the education sector. This crossed the false dichotomies that exist within education and developed relationships with teachers who previously would not have been listeners or contributors to the show. Following our most successful podcast ever with Paul Dix, I applied to host a weekly show on Teacher Hug radio, which would essentially be a version of the podcast. This community moved the podcast on immeasurably. The kindness, expertise and advice given graciously by the Teacher Hug team improved our production, the diversity of thought and the content of the show.

Ultimately the editing and scheduling became too much alongside the regular everyday job of a busy, by now, deputy head. I also became conscious that we were drifting away from the core of what made the podcast useful to listeners. We had stopped 'just talking to teachers' and had spent less time on research- and evidence-based practice. We had also largely moved away from giving listeners practical tips from serving teachers that they could use in the classroom. We had tried to be:

'. . . all things to all people.' 1 Corinthians 9:22

At the time of writing, we have gone back to basics in terms of content but, excitingly, have been chosen by Spotify to be an early adopter of their video podcast format. This means that rather than having to release a multi-format podcast on various providers, we can now offer listeners the chance to view guests as well as listen simultaneously. We feel that this will increase our appeal as teachers can now demonstrate as well as articulate their points. The medium will also lend itself to CPD sessions for staff, provided for free. This means 2022 will be an exciting step on our continuing journey of 'talking to teachers'.

Having taken you through the genesis and evolution of the podcast, here is our rationale for the book and how it can benefit you:

'The best that has been thought and said.' Matthew Arnold (1869)

Not for a minute am I comparing the output of an educational podcast to the classics of modern literature, but I have kept Arnold's words with me and they have provided the inspiration and the guidance for this book. An education book written by a teacher of over 20 years' standing may have some use. My perspectives on educational developments may be of note. My wisdom (such as it is) gained from working closely with some outstanding practitioners over a long career may help prevent others from making similar mistakes to my own. This book, however, is not that. This book is the accumulation of hundreds of hours of conversations with over 150 guests on the key topics in education, from CPD, behaviour, school leadership and pastoral care to the future of education. Reading this book may serve to increase your knowledge in much less than the three years it has taken me to accumulate this information and compile this book.

For each topic, I have distilled hours of relevant conversations into a set of clear, practical recommendations, translating the collective wisdom of the podcast guests into actionable advice for teachers, school leaders, governors and the wider profession. A key theme throughout is cutting through the binary debates that happen on social media in order to unite tribes and escape echo chambers. I hope that by exploring the thoughts and opinions of a wide range of podcast guests, you will find that there is more to unite us as educators than to divide us.

The advice draws upon my conversations with all the guests on the podcast to date, at the time of writing in early 2022. However, for each topic, I have selected a range of key expert guests whose contributions and thinking I am keen to explore in more detail. From Professor Michael Young and Professor Becky Allen to Dr Jill Berry, Aziza Ajak, Pritesh Raichura and Paul Dix, my hope is that this will set you off on an educational journey to the works of these luminaries in the world of education. I hope the book will serve as a reference text for study into the outputs of the featured educators, set up as it is with handy QR codes to directly reference their podcast episodes as you go along your journey.

How to use this book

Take a look at the table of contents and choose a topic that interests you or that you are working on at the moment, for example behaviour. Navigate to the chapter on behaviour and start reading! You can read the chapter from start to finish if you wish. Alternatively, I have included a handy overview at the start of each chapter listing out the key recommendations for that topic, along with page numbers, so you can jump straight to an idea that captures your attention if you prefer.

Throughout each chapter, you will find quotes from selected key podcast episodes with guests who are experts on the topic being explored. You can spot these quotes by looking for the Naylor's Natter microphone icon. If you would like to hear the expert discuss the topic in their own words, scan the QR code for their podcast episode and have a listen. If you would like to explore further, you can browse all available episodes from a variety of podcast providers, including Apple Podcasts, Google Podcasts and Spotify.

Each recommendation in the chapter has a 'Naylor's nuggets' feature, which distils the collective wisdom of the podcast guests into clear, practical tips and advice, and uses the author's experience as a teacher and school leader to make this useful to you in your classroom and in your context.

Instead of jumping straight to a particular topic, you are of course welcome to read the book straight through. If you are familiar with the podcast, you may wish to delve straight in and begin reading, pausing occasionally to revisit classic or long-forgotten conversations with guests you may like to hear again. The QR codes will be useful to support this.

Take action

Once you've read the book, it's time to bring your new learning to life.

- **Put it into practice.** Due to existential issues affecting schools, the core business of teaching has become naturally subjugated by national events. As someone who started a podcast with the express intention of professional development, I hope that this book and the associated conversations are used to change your teaching or school leadership practice, formulate policy and most importantly of all increase the life chances of the next generation of children.

- **Start a book club.** All of the expert guests I mention in the book (and many others besides) have written their own books about education. Why not start a book club in your department or school to encourage you and your colleagues to delve into these books further and discuss them together to help inform your collective practice?

- **Formulate a CPD programme.** As someone who has responsibility for the organisation of a professional development programme, I know how difficult this can be logistically, economically and organisationally. Whatever area it is that you are developing, there is a Naylor's Natter episode for you. It may even be the implementation of the programme that you have already settled on. The chapter titles will give you an overview, the nuggets will give you the key points and the episode links will give you free access to the minds of experts to help inform your CPD programme.

- **Get in touch.** If you would like to discuss the podcast, the topics raised in the book or any other educational topic with us, please get in touch on Twitter @naylorsnatter or through the contact form on our website at https://naylorsnatterpodcastjusttalkingtoteachers.wordpress.com.

1 The importance of continuing professional development

Chapter overview

There is no denying that the quantity and quality of continuing professional development (CPD) available to teachers has a direct correlation with school effectiveness and improvement. CPD for teachers used to mean a one-off INSET day at the beginning of September but it has to be so much more than that to have a real impact on practice. In this chapter we will delve into some key conversations on the podcast in order to examine how professional development has evolved over the years and how it can be delivered most effectively.

Recommendations:

Featuring podcast episodes with:

- **Dr Thomas Guskey**, July 2019
- **Dame Alison Peacock**, October 2019
- **Sir John Jones**, February 2021
- **Chris Moyse**, February 2020
- **Professor Sam Twiselton (with Emma Turner)**, February 2020
- **Dr Carl Hendrick and Professor Paul Kirschner**, April 2020

- **Pritesh Raichura**, May 2019
- **David Weston and Jack Worth**, January 2020
- **Simon Cox**, January 2021
- **Mary Myatt**, October 2020
- **Jonny Uttley (with Kathryn Morgan)**, April 2020
- **John Tomsett**, May 2020
- **Stephen Tierney**, August 2020

I never wanted to be a teacher. I was not steeped in the teaching profession: none of my family had been teachers and none of my friends had been teachers; in fact I did not know any teachers at all. Raised in a second-generation working-class household in Thatcher's Britain, education was given the utmost importance as a method of social mobility and economic improvement. I can distinctly remember to this day my father's words when I was choosing my options: 'You cannot go wrong with three sciences; you will always have a job.' This firm sense of direction was somewhat lost following my father's death whilst I was in the first year of a biology degree at university. This resulted in complete freedom of choice academically, spiritually, morally and in choice of occupation. Left alone to choose a career, I naturally gravitated to one of the few things I have been reasonably good at, namely the world of football. Now this is not some hard-luck story where a cruciate knee ligament injury curtailed the playing career of a young starlet. After all, this is an education book and not a football autobiography. I am telling you this to illustrate some of the points I want to address in this chapter regarding professional and personal development in education.

Having been identified as a potential coach of elite footballers through many weeks of observation of my Saturday morning soccer camp, I was given the opportunity to come on board and coach Wigan Athletic's under 14s. Now this is no mean feat for a 21-year-old fresh out of university. I quickly realised the world of football had a clear focus on improvement (of both the coaches and the players) and the methods of evaluation were extremely regular, namely every Sunday morning. Professional development was prioritised by the Football Association, the football club, and the coaches. This professional development was underpinned by years of accumulated evidence and expertise. There was a culture of sharing best practice, either anecdotally or through the widespread borrowing of books between the coaches, and the watching of endless hours of videos of the leading practitioners of the time.

The professional development was sustained over time and, even better, informed by evidence and expert knowledge.

All good professional development also includes collaboration and expert challenge. Every Saturday morning whilst coaching at the JJB Soccer Dome in Wigan, I would engage in conversation with a likeable and knowledgeable parent at the gate of pitch one. We would chat regularly about Everton's dismal performance at the weekend along with developments in the world of coaching, tactics and professional learning. These conversations came to define the next chapter in my fledgling career. Older readers will be aware of the push in the early 2000s of the then Labour government to recruit as many teachers as possible to help staff their Building Schools for the Future project. Having been fortunate enough to gain the degree that my father had guided me into, I was suitably qualified to embark on teacher training. The coaching continued at Wigan and subsequently other academies, as did the collaboration and expert challenge, not only through the leadership of the football club but also through the conversations I had about teaching with that one particular parent at the gate of pitch one.

In this chapter, I want to discuss four key recommendations for CPD that were illustrated during my time at Wigan Athletic and that have, more recently, been discussed at length on the podcast with various guests and in specific relation to teaching staff. As you read, think about your own experiences of professional development: what has worked well for you and what hasn't worked quite so well? What would you like to see more of and what could be dropped? If you're a school leader, consider what's on offer to teachers in your department or school. Is the CPD you're providing having a positive impact on practice and, if not, what could be improved?

Recommendation 1: CPD should be sustained over time, particularly for ECTs

It's August 2002 and I am now settled into my first teaching job. I am a newly qualified teacher (NQT, as it was known then) in a science department of vastly experienced colleagues, some of whom have been sitting in the same seat in the staffroom since the Bay City Rollers topped the charts. Professional development was not a term in everyday use at the turn of the millennium. INSET days, twilights and staff meetings focused on routine administration and widespread apathy. Newly qualified teachers were rather expected to develop subject knowledge, pedagogy and practice through assimilation or diffusion in conversations on

Friday evening lock-ins at the local pub. We were of course assigned mentors to help us harness the collective wisdom of the profession. My mentor meetings in the early days somewhat resembled the start of Matthew Kelly's *Stars in Their Eyes*. Upon opening the door to my mentor's office, I was met with plumes of smoke as he emerged from behind the desk: 'Tonight Philip, I am going to be your mentor and I am going to teach you the ways to survive in this profession.' These nuggets of advice involved urban myth, legend, and some salient advice. One of the most memorable to this day was: 'Ignore any phone call or message the first time; if it is important, they will always find you.' This is not advice I would give to any professional.

Alongside twilights and department meetings we had the annual INSET day. Well, I say day, but we actually did nine 'til 12 and the students came in at one o'clock for the afternoon. These days usually involved an expert in the field selling themselves as a provider of training. These people, whilst mostly well-meaning, undoubtedly sincere and honest, were usually the provider of edutainment. My favourite example of one of these INSET training days was provided by a gentleman who asked us to pick a card at random from his selection of wild animals. He then asked us to describe in detail how we could channel the characteristics of said animal into our teacher persona. We had to design posters, raps and act out a scene to illustrate our channelling. After a day of toe-curling embarrassment, I was still struggling with my inner wildebeest!

It is hard to describe professional learning in the early 2000s without straying into well-trodden anecdotes around Brain Gym®, thinking hats, learning styles and other now happily debunked education myths. The acts on the circuit had well-honed, often inspirational training sessions designed to confuse and inspire teachers in equal measure, but in the words of David Weston, CEO of the Teacher Development Trust, when I interviewed him for the podcast:

 'Learning is not the same as listening to people sharing great ideas.'
David Weston

Many of the ideas and strategies that were shared were immediately implemented. Quite often in every classroom, on the very next day, you would see that particular approach being adopted, that idea being piloted, or that strategy being deployed. By the end of the week the school budget had been spent on sticky notes and flipchart paper. The students looked dazed and permanently confused from another high-energy learning experience. Dr Thomas Guskey, one of the leading experts in professional development, put it like this when I asked him about one-off, standalone CPD sessions:

 'I know that as a teacher, when our school leader would go to a conference, we would always be concerned because we knew that that leader was going to come back with all sorts of new things they wanted to try, simply because they had heard a presenter there.' Dr Thomas Guskey

To hear more from **Dr Thomas Guskey**, scan this QR code.

These sessions tended not to lead to long-term change as they were certainly not sustained over time. Other than these standalone days, professional learning was not prioritised by school leadership overall.

It seems there was something missing not only in my early career but also in the early career of many teachers. In a natter with Dame Alison Peacock, we unpicked the lack of professional development and mentoring available for early career teachers (ECTs). This is something that The Chartered College of Teaching are working hard to improve for current entrants to the profession:

 'Now, when I was an NQT I was observed three times in that year; but if there had been a riot going on in my class, then people would have noticed! There is almost a sense of "yes, she can do it" or "no, perhaps he can't", without any sort of identifying of the skills involved. What are the strategies that you need? There are lots of skills and strategies that we have to be much better at sharing.' Dame Alison Peacock

To hear more from **Dame Alison Peacock**, scan this QR code.

So, how can we share those skills and strategies with teachers, especially ECTs, in a more sustainable way?

What does CPD sustained over time look like?

I remember one particular INSET day when I made my way to school head to toe in nylon thanks to the high street's budget tailoring, bursting with excitement and anticipation of another academic year. Upon my arrival, through clouds of smoke, to the pigeonhole in the corner of the smoking room, I picked up the agenda for the INSET morning. Our keynote speaker was to be renowned headteacher and educator Sir John Jones. I remember being quite excited by the presence of a knight of the realm in lovely Burnley on a late summer's morning.

Sitting in the back row of the staffroom, sandwiched between the head of science completing her knitting and a snoozing senior member of staff, I craned my neck to catch a glimpse of the baronet as he strode majestically into our staffroom. At that time, my youthful eyes were glasses-free, so I rubbed them cartoon-style to make sure that the knight in shining pinstripes was indeed the same parent who had stood watching my football coaching and offering advice for the preceding three years. My eyes were not deceiving me. He was indeed the parent at the gate of pitch one.

'Sir John is going to talk to you about magic weaving,' purred the headteacher. 'You will discover how his experience of leadership in some of the most challenging areas in the country can help you to weave some magic of your own in your classroom.'

This INSET just felt different from the usual professional development I had experienced thus far. This was the first time that I felt as if my personal and professional development had been a priority for the school. Here in front of us was a practising headteacher working in challenging circumstances, prepared to share his insights with us, to collaborate and to provide us with some challenge. This CPD has stayed with me some 20 years later. When I interviewed Sir John for the podcast, I asked him why he had not revealed to me that he was a headteacher, let alone a knight of the realm, when we stood together next to the football pitch. He offered this humble explanation:

'*People are interested in who you are; this is so much more important than what you are or what you've done.*' **Sir John Jones**

Sir John's INSET presentation focused on what CPD really is and really means. The work he had engaged in at the gate of the football field was professional development for me; the fact that he returned to it every week made it continuous. Regularity was missing from the training and meetings of my early career. This is a theme we have touched on in the podcast, notably in a conversation with Chris Moyse who talked about his approach to professional growth:

To hear more from **Sir John Jones**, scan this QR code.

'What always got me about CPD, that three-letter acronym, is that we often forget what the letters stand for: continuing professional development, which in my head is something that you continually do rather than something you do in the odd twilight.' Chris Moyse

Continuity is an essential aspect of CPD, particularly in those first few years of a teacher's professional life. The best way to deliver on this is to provide regular CPD that focuses on developing a particular area of practice sustained over time.

To hear more from **Chris Moyse**, scan this QR code.

The Early Career Framework

Things are of course hugely different now for new entrants to the profession. No longer do ECTs need to rely on motivational speakers, perfunctory twilight sessions or edutainment training days. The Early Career Framework (ECF) has plotted a course for new teachers to navigate their development through the crucial early years in the profession. The ECF recognises that too often new teachers have not enjoyed the support they need to thrive, nor have they had adequate time to devote to their professional development.

Professor Sam Twiselton in a natter with Emma Turner talked about the importance of a framework and a structure to professional learning, particularly in a climate of high expectations for new teachers. Sam noted that it is important for leaders to prioritise CPD in order to support their new teachers, reduce stress and help ECTs to stay in the profession for longer.

To hear more from **Professor Sam Twiselton**, scan this QR code.

'New teachers are expected to hit the ground running and be that perfect teacher. Expectations on them are very high. That creates stress; that creates workload problems. And we know that the outcome of that is more and more teachers leave. [The ECF will provide] at least a minimum of three years of ongoing, high-quality support and development. And not only is that a really good thing in itself, because it's recognising formally that you're continuing to learn, and you need that support, it is also, I think, potentially changing the whole narrative.' Professor Sam Twiselton

Naylor's nuggets

- CPD isn't just about presenters sharing ideas in a one-off, standalone session. By its very nature CPD should be delivered regularly and should focus on developing a particular area of practice over time.

- This approach is particularly important for early career teachers, who need ongoing high-quality support and development. The new Early Career Framework should be utilised as a tool to support this.

- Leaders can sustain this development by prioritising professional learning with time, status and funding.

Recommendation 2: Evidence-based and research-informed CPD is most effective

Those who can, teach. This slogan was splashed across billboards, was pumped out by the television, and covered whole pages of newspapers in the early 2000s. A teacher recruitment crisis was beginning to bite and a sizable percentage of the profession was leaving or retiring. The Labour government's solution to this was to put money into making teaching a more attractive career through financial rewards, coupled with the idea that it could attract professionals who would like a career change. These initiatives were commendable and did lead to an increase in the number of people entering teacher training colleges up and down the country.

However, a second narrative developed in the profession at this time, which was not explicitly linked to the slogan and in my view (then and now) was potentially damaging in the long term for teachers. I had graduated with a biology degree, not a great biology degree, but a biology degree nonetheless. I felt I had a good handle on the essential concepts and principles of biology. However, the narrative was the idea that good teachers can teach anything, that pedagogy in some way trumps deep subject knowledge. Relationships and engagement were prioritised over opportunities for pupils to learn and master the critical components of your subject. Within this context, I was put through a qualification to become what was called at the time an Advanced Skills Teacher (AST). I had to undergo assessments, provide evidence of exceptional exam results, and deliver two or three model lessons to be assessed by an external examiner. I was very fortunate to pass the exam and privileged to be appointed as the aforementioned AST. I was struck at the time (and continue to be so now) by the focus on the methods of delivery in the classroom at the expense of detailed subject knowledge. I am ashamed to admit I had a complete lack of understanding of the process of learning. Nowhere on this assessment was there any explanation of how we learn or the evidence behind this. It was not until around 2017 that I did any studying into how learning happens, as I discussed with Dr Carl Hendrick and Professor Paul Kirschner on Naylor's Natter. Carl recounted his experience of this period:

'I can remember being shown lessons 15 years ago, where the whole lesson was basically trying to get students to kind of stumble across right answers or to write things in spite of themselves. So, they're either some sort of treasure hunt, or some sort of delusion of active learning.' Dr Carl Hendrick

The role of the AST did have its good points in that it allowed progression for a classroom teacher. The opportunity to move through the ranks of both pay and status without having to take on leadership and management responsibilities was a valuable stepping stone. These managerial responsibilities can often detract from the part of the job that teachers came into the profession to do. This leaves them forever compromised between classroom delivery and the competing demands of school leadership. Nevertheless, as an AST I became an expert at delivering out-of-the-box, one-off, 'show-pony' lessons involving

To hear more from **Dr Carl Hendrick** and **Professor Paul Kirschner**, scan this QR code.

tightly focused lesson plans, enthusiastically delivered mini plenaries every ten minutes, assessment for learning opportunities and three-part lessons. I became a hollow performer.

I have recounted this story on other podcasts, but it is something that sticks with me from this period of my career. Exiting the classroom after another 'rent an outstanding lesson' delivered to a classroom full of excited Year 7s and underwhelmed science teachers, I happened to be parading down the corridor resembling an extra from *The Apprentice* at the same time as the vastly experienced geography teacher; we were both making our way to the staffroom for our afternoon coffee. The conversation with Michael began with British-weather-based pleasantries before segueing into a Road to Damascus-style conversation which lingers some 15 years later.

'It's all been round once and it'll all come round again,' deadpanned Michael as a deliberate bait to a flash young sod in a pinstripe suit.

'Go on then, I'll bite. What will? These ideas? What ideas?'

Now rather than bore the reader with the entire conversation, the gist of it can be summarised quite easily as follows. Michael had seen education fads come and go, education secretaries change every 18 months, pedagogies and practices become fashionable and then fade or face a backlash. In the face of huge change, he had been stoic throughout his teaching career. His unwavering belief in the solid principles of common-sense education remained. He elucidated on this rainy Tuesday afternoon in Burnley: 'Every lesson I'm at my door; I say good morning to the students. I ask about their brothers and sisters, their parents and family. I always start with a quiz based on last lesson, which they mark themselves. They do not give me the marks, but I can get a feel for what they know and what they don't and then I adapt my lesson accordingly. I know my subject inside out; I continue to study it and I am hugely passionate about it. We have a curriculum; it is called a textbook and we work our way through the textbook every lesson, every week. I set them tasks, we mark the tasks, I offer feedback. None of those fancy stamps that you are using. I find out what they don't know, and I teach them that.'

Michael went on to explain how he had developed the best way to tell stories to illustrate and give examples, explanations and demonstrations in geography. He detailed how he knows which bits of geography will be easy and which bits his students will find difficult. He expounded his theory of teacher talk: he talks a lot because he knows his subject inside out. High standards of behaviour were demanded and then became expected. He ran his own detentions and inexplicably (to my naivety) the students really seemed to enjoy these lessons.

As a 24-year-old Advanced Skills Teacher, I was incredulous: textbooks? I spent last summer throwing those into a skip to make room for more shelves of flipchart paper, whiteboard pens and sticky notes. A test when they come into the lesson? Everybody knows that lessons should start with the starter, then a mini plenary, then another short activity, then another mini plenary and then a main activity. Every lesson should continue to follow the lesson plan regardless of whether students seem to have learned the content or not – we must complete the curriculum! I did not need to know my subject in depth and the students did not necessarily need to know my subject. Any information that we needed we could find on Google. Ultimately all we needed to be able to do was to fill out the blanks on a differentiated worksheet to prove that we'd made progress.

This approach that was being pushed through ASTs, consultants and teacher training institutions did not allow for many of the 'common sense' approaches that Michael explained. This was a theme I picked up in an early Naylor's Natter with Pritesh Raichura who is Head of Science at Michaela Community School. Pritesh trained in the early 2010s and reflected:

'When I was training to be a teacher, inquiry-based learning was definitely pushed and less teacher talk was definitely pushed. And I think that when you're training and you're starting off as a teacher, you quickly realise it is quite tricky because then you don't guide the pupils that you have in front of you; you don't get the results that you want.' Pritesh Raichura

In an episode with Jack Worth of the NFER, David Weston teased out the idea of professional autonomy and the fact that certain ideas were and are prevalent in the profession. David and Jack discussed whether teachers have autonomy over their choice of professional development and Jack stated:

 'What was a real surprise... was that autonomy over professional development goals was particularly low. So only 23 per cent said they had a lot of autonomy in

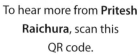

To hear more from **Pritesh Raichura,** scan this QR code.

this area. And 38 per cent said they had even none or a little influence over their professional development goals, which seemed to be not quite fitting with where we might expect it to be.' Jack Worth

Jack raised this as a concern, saying that having autonomy over CPD was strongly associated with increased job satisfaction, which in turn correlates with retention. It's therefore important that teachers are trusted to manage their own professional development, set their own goals and targets, take ownership of the areas of practice they need to improve and make decisions about the direction in which they want their careers to progress.

Listening to and working with experienced colleagues (like Michael) is a great starting point to help teachers to develop powerful examples, explanations,

To hear more from **David Weston** and **Jack Worth,** scan this QR code.

demonstrations and subject-specific analogies in the areas they need and want to develop. This can also help teachers to understand common misconceptions in their subjects and help pupils to overcome these. To aid this development, leaders should prioritise professional learning for teachers and non-teaching staff. Teachers should be given the opportunity to study the essential knowledge, skills and key concepts of their subject discipline and constantly refresh this in line with recent developments. Middle and senior leaders should also enable departments and staff teams to share knowledge, expertise and best practice both formally and informally to enable them to learn from one another.

Becoming a research-informed practitioner

'Do you want to help run a Research School?' This was the opening gambit of a conversation in our headteacher's office in 2017.

Leaping forward some 15 years from my NQT year, my career had stagnated somewhat following ten years of assistant headship in many different pastoral iterations and the time was right for something new.

'A Research School is a new concept; we've been asked to head one up and you are going down to York next week to find out a little bit more.'

I was very fortunate at the time to be chosen to work alongside the marvellous Mr Simon Cox whose persona and personality were perfectly suited to the world of evidence and research. Simon was, as ever, much further down the road than I was, having had his finger on the pulse of developments in education over the last few years. He was well prepared to take on the responsibility of running a Research School as we discussed on the very first episode of Naylor's Natter.

'I was becoming more aware of evidence and research. I think there's been a big push over the past few years, moving away from what can be very dry academic journals towards things that were a lot more readable for teachers and a lot more accessible and relevant to the day job.' Simon Cox

To hear more from **Simon Cox,** scan this QR code.

We headed down to York for the inaugural conference of Research Schools. Opening with the keynote on the first morning was my personal favourite Education Secretary (the person whose signature still adorns my QTS certificate) Baroness Estelle Morris. Baroness Morris proceeded to dazzle us with her keynote speech, which included a memorable quote about Research Schools. She postulated that they were the worst-named institution in education, as they were not going to conduct any academic research. They should have been called Evidence Schools as the primary job would be to disseminate evidence into schools; to put it into the hands of teachers and school leaders and to make it usable for teachers in their own classrooms. Apparently, however, Evidence Schools is not as marketable a name and it does not get the creative juices flowing in quite the same way.

So, suddenly I am the Assistant Director of a Research School. I can have my name on my office door in copper-plate bold writing. There was only one small problem, readers: you could write everything I knew about academic research on the back of a postage stamp with a rather large marker pen. Academic research and evidence up to this point had been something that went on in universities. Something that I may have glanced at during my PGCE and a rather stilted, dull and detached form of potential learning, much less sexy than the aforementioned educational consultants and edutainment.

As we moved our way through the first morning, we listened to more wonderful presentations that really started to pique my professional curiosity. I may be overstating this as a life-changing experience, but it certainly changed the next few years in my professional life. On that scorching, clammy morning in July 2017, I really started to question everything that I had done up to this point, both as a teacher and a leader. Questions popped into my head as I listened attentively to the speakers. Why do we do assessments in the way that we do now? Is it because that is the way the school has always done it, or it is the way the 'outstanding' school down the road does it? I remembered meetings where ideas were discussed and accepted based on a hunch, impulse or bias. Whole-school strategies based on what had been seen on Twitter or (I appreciate the irony here) what had been read in a book. I had never heard any evidence-based discussions up to this point and I do not think I had ever asked on what basis decisions were made. Lamentably few national strategy decisions ever involved the accumulated wisdom of the teachers and leaders in schools. Even more shockingly, I do not think I ever questioned whether my own practice was effective. I was doing things because I had been told to or because this is the way that things had always been done. David Weston, CEO of the Teacher Development Trust, had a similar experience earlier in his career:

'I started reading research and once I discovered the rich research about how teachers can improve it blew my mind. I thought if I'd had this throughout my career this would have been amazing.' **David Weston**

At the Blackpool Research School launch, we were extremely fortunate to have Sir Kevan Collins (who, at the time, was the CEO of the EEF) come up to Blackpool to do our opening evening. In his keynote, Sir Kevan talked about how teachers can use evidence-informed practice in the classroom and how it was almost our moral imperative to study and to use the best in academic research. Sir Kevan told the story of how he started teaching some 30 years previously. He talked openly about the two lines of children in the corridor of his first school. One line turns left to go to his class and one turns right to go to Sue. He articulated with great integrity how one turn could lead to the accumulated wisdom of 20 years in the classroom and the betterment of the life chances of these disadvantaged London children in Sue's capable hands. The other students were to be taught to the best of his ability by a young, inexperienced Mr Collins. At our launch evening, Sir Kevan recounted this story and along with it some important information on the way the profession should move forward with evidence-informed teaching. He chose the teaching of reading as an example of where the evidence is strong.

> 'Every teacher has a right to know that stuff and every child has a right to high-quality teaching.' Sir Kevan Collins at the launch of Blackpool Research School

He went on to discuss the alternatives to evidence: do we use luck, throw around enough ideas and see what sticks, or borrow and steal ideas from other schools, adopting them wholesale to fix an as yet undefined issue? Personally, I felt that many schools were doing things as an accountability exercise to ensure that the Ofsted banner could be hung outside the school gates (a seemingly trivial but often financially essential grading for the survival of the school). These technocratic approaches are often not justified by evidence, for example, the widely used but poorly evidenced triple marking.

> 'What is the consequence of not using evidence? Huge variation within and between schools; the luck of the draw. You wouldn't accept this in medicine: your GP makes it up and this doctor uses evidence.' Sir Kevan Collins at the launch of Blackpool Research School

This last quote really started to crystallise my thinking about the benefits of using evidence and research, especially in the context of my school. Many schools in Blackpool were working under challenging circumstances, with Ofsted grades to match. School leaders were under intense scrutiny and huge pressure to make rapid change. The challenges were wide ranging, from teacher recruitment to pupils' academic performance and from curriculum choice to exclusions.

Analysing this from a slightly distanced vantage, it seemed that at the time the preferred approach to rapid school improvement was to take existing pockets of subjective excellence in schools (whether that be teachers, departments or experts) and then simply replicate these. Parachuting them from one establishment or organisation into another, you copy them and then push staff to work even harder. This would also be supported by huge initiatives to augment and supplement the work already going on in school. These initiatives could be breakfast classes, after-school catch-up sessions, weekend classes, holiday classes... the list was endless. There was also the pressure to measure more to evidence this rapid improvement. This could be both internally and externally, in the vain hope that the system could begin to improve itself.

So how do we go about getting research into teachers' hands and supporting them to use it? It's not easy in a system already overloaded with endless new initiatives and a culture of quick fix and rapid turnaround. When I spoke with Mary Myatt for the second time about her book *Back on Track* (2020), she talked about how she also felt it was important to stop doing things before embarking on anything new:

 'Some of that I believe can be trimmed back and can be cut back. One of the things I explore in the book is: why are we doing things routinely? Because we've just always done them, and it's making us feel busy. It's made us feel that we've done something, yes, but how has it added or made a difference to what our core purpose is meant to be, which is giving children lots of interesting knowledge?' Mary Myatt

As teachers and school leaders, it's essential to cut back on some of the things that are filling up time but having no impact on outcomes. Take a step back and evaluate whether what you are spending your time on is making a difference to your pupils' learning. If not, it may be necessary to lose these practices in order to divert your energy elsewhere. Teachers need time to engage fully and critically with available research and evidence and to implement it in the classroom. A great place to start is the EEF's Teaching and Learning Toolkit

To hear more from **Mary Myatt**, scan this QR code.

(https://educationendowmentfoundation.org.uk/education-evidence/teaching-learning-toolkit), which provides readable and practical summaries of available evidence in education. Setting up a reading group or a discussion group with colleagues is also an efficient way of covering a lot of ground: each individual can read one piece of research and then summarise the key points for the rest of the group. You can then discuss how the research could be implemented in your context. The EEF's 'Guide to implementation' (2019a) is a useful resource to help school leaders implement new ideas more effectively (you can access it at https://educationendowmentfoundation.org.uk/education-evidence/guidance-reports/implementation).

Naylor's nuggets

- To support your professional development as a teacher, it's essential to engage fully and critically with available research and evidence.
- Discuss research and evidence with colleagues and consider how you can implement it in your classroom.
- Evaluate the impact of your practice on the outcomes of your students.
- School leaders should ensure that professional development is underpinned by robust evidence and expertise. Examine the available evidence and research and utilise the EEF implementation guide.
- Make fewer decisions based on ideology, hunch or habit.
- Remember that context is key.

Recommendation 3: The best CPD involves collaboration and expert challenge

Blackpool has been designated as an opportunity area since 2017. This has brought in much-needed finance to help the educational and life chances of some of the most disadvantaged children in the country. Another project that has provided support is the Teacher Development Trust's CPD Excellence Hubs Programme (TLIF). As I was fortunate enough to have extensive connections through the town (having worked on cross-school initiatives), it was felt that my powers of persuasion may help to increase collaboration between schools and I became an expert advisor for the Blackpool Hub.

The next conversation is one of those chance life moments that set you on a totally different pathway. Inspired by the words of Baz Luhrmann in *Everybody's Free (To Wear Sunscreen)*, 'I always think that the real changes in life are things that blindside you 'some idle Tuesday.' This particular Tuesday in November, our next guest speaker was moving from her keynote into a more detailed presentation. Being a professional at the technological cutting-edge, she had an iPad Pro and wanted it beamed onto our screen. As I am a bit of a technical geek, I had the piece of equipment needed to get the presentation up and running. In the interim, our esteemed guest asked about the TDT project and Blackpool as an opportunity area. I explained my role in both and the teething issues we had encountered. I had an obligation to get research into the hands of practitioners and to convince school leaders to make their decisions based on the best evidence. I also shared the vision for the CPD Excellence Hub; how we had privileged access to all senior leaders across the town to work with them on designing their CPD programme for the year. As I elucidated our vision, I could feel the cogs slowly turning in my mind. Our esteemed guest responded with:

> *'So, you have evidence-based practice and academic research that you struggle to get into schools, but you have privileged access to all senior leaders to design their CPD programmes without an obvious focus for their professional development.'*

You do not have to be Columbo to work out what came next. This brings us to our next aspect of CPD, which is that professional development should include collaboration and expert challenge. I have deliberately put this alongside the previous nugget that professional development should be underpinned by robust evidence and expertise. In my experience, collaboration can include stakeholders working together on unproven, non-evidence-based strategies that they think may work or that have worked previously or that work in their friend's school or that they have seen on Twitter. We discussed and agreed the idea of putting the two projects together: ensuring that any CPD was underpinned by robust evidence and expertise, while also working together within and between schools to ensure that all the professional development undertaken included collaboration and expert challenge.

Collaboration and expert challenge are often built into a school's 'performance management' process. Teachers are always striving to get better, but as a middle leader I came to dread the annual appraisal season, which invariably went something like this:

- Analyse exam results in detail: The post-mortem begins and challenging results targets are set for the year ahead.

- Set generic and vague targets in November: Targets include sweeping whole-school change, for example, improve teaching and learning this year; improve attendance of Pupil Premium boys; narrow the disadvantage gap; ensure that all lessons are outstanding; reduce fixed-term exclusions.

- Attach a data objective to these targets that is illogical and unattainable: An example would be that 54.3 per cent of Pupil Premium boys will achieve a Grade 4 in science this year. 92 per cent of all observed lessons will be outstanding. There will be no fixed-term exclusions.

- Cascade targets through leadership, phase, department and classroom.

- Observe each teacher at least three times to see if these targets are being met before Easter.

- Write up mountains of paperwork in triplicate to evidence the process.

- Revisit in the following November and decide on pay progression.

To ensure these targets were prioritised by the school and teachers, they were quite often attached to teachers' pay. In order to make the next pay scale, teachers would have to jump through the hoops strategically placed for them by school leaders and measured by the performance of their students. There also used to be a specific target around teachers' own personal development. Often this was a course or a qualification such as an NPQ or equivalent leadership qualification. There was usually little flexibility in personal development, particularly for part-time and support staff.

Professional development had become at best a box-ticking exercise and at worst a punitive accountability measure. The process inadvertently resulted in loss of teachers from the profession. One of the first targets for the new Research School and CPD Excellence Hub in Blackpool was to establish a single commitment for teachers to get better at teaching. The vehicle for this seems naturally to be a conversation about professional development.

The good news is that we are seeing a shift in the use of performance-related pay and Jonny Uttley, CEO of The Education Alliance (TEAL) Multi-Academy Trust, was forthright in his views when speaking to Kathryn Morgan on the podcast:

'I think performance-related pay was probably the biggest mistake the system ever made. It discourages innovation. I think if you link performance management or performance-related pay in school, you introduce an incentive to set a low target. And it takes up an awful lot of time, it takes up an awful lot of emotional energy, and it has no benefit whatsoever.' Jonny Uttley

He went on:

'So, without the constraint of performance-related pay and conventional performance management, [it's about] actually having an ongoing conversation across the year: how are you going to get better at your job? Then linking people into evidence- and subject-specific CPD.' Jonny Uttley

John Tomsett, the co-author (with Jonny) of the book *Putting Staff First* (2020), flipped the system of performance management on its head in his school. John removed punitive data targets, allowing staff the autonomy to choose their own development areas and encouraging professional collaboration and ongoing professional development.

John and Jonny have worked very hard to establish cultures in their schools where they put staff first and this is something we will cover in detail in Chapter 3 on leadership. The crucial factor in the context of CPD is that every teacher in their charge accepts that as a professional they have a duty to improve their practice. John and Jonny have both removed data-driven targets and focus instead on the quality of teaching. This doesn't mean not paying heed to any data. It simply means being aware of any measurable improvement but not becoming obsessed with it. Teachers select an area of practice they would like to improve on based on their performance analysis and not diluted from the whole-school development plan. In John's words from his conversation with me on the podcast:

To hear more from **Jonny Uttley**, scan this QR code.

'You make sure what [teachers] are working on is derived from their analysis of the results of their students. And then you teach them how to evaluate the impact of their interventions. It's not hard to do.' John Tomsett

If lessons are observed this is done within the culture of professional development. Any observer will provide feedback solely focused on improving colleagues' teaching. Teachers may even begin to enjoy professional conversations with colleagues on an ad hoc basis, not just at the normal appraisal times. This can provide colleagues with an opportunity to challenge each other's thinking. Expertise runs deep throughout the teaching profession and can be specific to phase or subject context and category.

As John puts it himself in his blog, expert challenge 'gets the balance between pressure and high standards about right *most of the time*' (Tomsett, 2015). Most importantly of all it leads to improved student progress, which is, after all, our moral obligation as teachers and public servants. John gave me confidence in our conversation that a system like the one in his school would be possible in any school:

'If you're really bold about it, and you're very supportive of staff, I think you can set those [systems] up really well.' John Tomsett

Ready and armed with evidence- and research-based CPD that had a clear focus on changing practice, I headed out to meet with senior leaders as part of my leadership roles for the Blackpool Research School and the CPD Excellence Hub. I was welcomed enthusiastically but warily by headteachers, who listened to my pitch on how we could collaborate and provide each other with expert challenge. There was one small issue: education is often awash with initiatives, particularly in areas of high disadvantage or where achievement has been highlighted as below what is required

To hear more from **John Tomsett**, scan this QR code.

or expected. Headteachers' inboxes and meeting schedules are full to the brim with 'experts' like me promising the next great silver bullet that will hit the target of rapid improvement. Leaders in these circumstances are quite understandably looking for a quick-fix, high-intensity intervention that will keep the wolves from the door.

The difference with the Blackpool Research School and CPD Excellence Hub was that they involved a three-year programme with regular fortnightly meetings and the requisite funding to facilitate this. In other words, this professional development, unlike the quick turnarounds, would be sustained over time.

It was around this time that the EEF released what, in my view, is the seminal work on school improvement; namely their implementation guide. This allowed us to put evidence to work. Once senior leaders had been convinced of the voracity of the project, we set about using the implementation guide as the basis for our initial conversations, which I can whole-heartedly recommend to all readers.

I discussed the issue of initiative overload and the pressures senior leaders are under in a podcast with Stephen Tierney. Stephen is a hugely experienced senior leader who has worked for the majority of his career in areas of high disadvantage. He has always had the force of his convictions to do the best for the young people in his charge and has not veered from this course throughout his 16 years of headship. He talked about how he has seen ideas, policies, fads and fashions come and go over his tenure and said:

 'If an idea isn't a nine out of ten then don't do it.' Stephen Tierney

The idea that senior leaders could stop doing something is so counterintuitive to the prevailing narrative. Teachers and leaders are expected to be like Boxer in Orwell's *Animal Farm*: always working harder and harder to the point of exhaustion. In areas of disadvantage, teachers are expected to work longer hours and more strenuously to (in some way) mitigate the educational disadvantage. There is a feeling that leaders should be intervening more and working harder as something must be done. The notion that senior leaders could raise their heads from the everyday issues and in the words of the implementation guide 'prioritise appropriately' was a revelation to all the heads I spoke with. I asked one school leader whether their intense Year 11 catch-up programme, encompassing the following initiatives, had made any difference:

To hear more from **Stephen Tierney**, scan this QR code.

- mandatory after-school catch-up
- half-term master classes
- breakfast revision classes

- weekend trips to a water park
- moving teachers from Key Stage 3 classes to take Year 11 'off timetable' two weeks before exams to concentrate on English and maths.

The data provided showed that exam results hadn't moved in the last three years, despite in their words 'throwing the kitchen sink at it'. Anecdotal evidence had also seen an increase in teachers moving on, an increase in low-level disruption in Key Stage 3 and a culture of accountability creeping in. 'If it isn't working, then why are you doing it?' seemed an obvious but impertinent question at this point. The scales fell from their eyes with the dawning realisation that there was another way. 'Well, we have to do something to become a good school.'

The idea that professional development should be sustained over time needs brave leadership. It needs leaders who prioritise CPD, devoting adequate time, providing commensurate funding and dropping any initiatives that clearly aren't working. This, along with a developmental culture, is integral to meaningful collaboration.

Naylor's nuggets

- Teachers (particularly early career teachers) can develop as professionals by:
  o having access to high-quality CPD which allows collaboration with other teachers
  o having and being given time to stop doing things and prioritise recovery and rest
  o understanding that support from the school leadership is a right.
- Collaborating to share the work of planning and preparation is crucial to a teacher's development.
- Leaders can aid this development by:
  o ensuring that professional development includes collaboration at all levels
  o prioritising professional development
  o seeking and encouraging expert challenge.

Recommendation 4: Evaluating CPD is more than a tick-box exercise

Coming to the end of the CPD Excellence Hub project in 2020, I had cause to reflect on whether we had achieved any of the targets set. In evaluating CPD previously (and coming full circle to the anecdote that started this chapter), we used to complete evaluation sheets at the end of each session to give feedback to the presenter and the school on the effectiveness of the session. These sheets were often more of a reflection of the quality of the buffet, the temperature of the room or the wit and personality of the presenter. These factors undoubtedly have their place and basic human needs must be catered for, but evaluation of CPD needs to be much more than a tick-box exercise at the end of a twilight session.

In one of my favourite podcasts, I had the pleasure of talking with Dr Thomas Guskey about his five-level model for evaluating CPD. He told me about its origins in the work of Donald Kirkpatrick. Kirkpatrick wrote in the 1950s about evaluating professional development programmes, primarily in business. Kirkpatrick developed a model that looked at four different levels or types of outcomes that could be considered. He labelled the four levels: reactions, learning, behaviour and results. As Dr Guskey described:

'Reaction was just how the employees would regard the training. Learning was what they actually developed from it, the new skills and the particular data. Behaviour had to do with their on-the-job performance; and results from the Kirkpatrick model focused primarily on the improvement in productivity.'
Dr Thomas Guskey

Dr Guskey took this model and added a fifth level. This new level focused on the organisation in which the teacher would be working, something we have covered in the previous recommendation on the importance of leaders prioritising CPD. Guskey discussed his five-level model:

'The five-level model dealt with the reactions: how people regard that initial training experience or their learning experiences. Second is the learning: what they gain, how it influences their knowledge and the skills that they have. Third is organisational support and change. Level four dealt with implementation: did

they use these ideas and use them with fidelity? And then finally, we looked at the impact on students.' Dr Thomas Guskey

The CPD sessions that so often used to start an academic year (like those I discussed at the beginning of the chapter) were planned from the standpoint of having something to *do* with teachers during a session. We now focused on how this training would help teachers to accomplish more with their students. Dr Guskey and I shared our experience of school leaders going to a conference and coming back with all sorts of new ideas that they wanted to try, whether there was evidence to support the ideas or not. The ideas were being made to fit the school rather than some evaluation of current practice taking place in order to decide what is needed. Dr Guskey advised:

'I think it's the change in our focus, pressing teachers to be more thoughtful about focusing their planning in terms of the learning outcomes of their students. We need to do the same for professional learning: we need to plan it by first focusing on what impact we want to have on students and what evidence we will trust.' Dr Thomas Guskey

Talking to Dr Guskey highlights the importance of planning CPD to improve student outcomes. The development of the teacher's skills and knowledge are crucial to this as quality of teaching makes the biggest difference to student outcomes. Guskey again highlights the importance of support from leadership and the prioritisation of CPD. He rightly raises awareness of the 'lethal mutation' of a seemingly good idea and its nullification through fidelity to the approach or approaches outlined. Dr Guskey's work also still takes heed of the importance of a positive reaction to a presenter or idea and the Maslow's hierarchy of needs, without which no idea will come to fruition. But these are just a handful of the factors that need to be evaluated in order to ascertain the long-term impact of CPD.

Naylor's nuggets

- Start planning CPD with the end in mind: evaluate what you want to achieve from this CPD and consider what impact this will have on student outcomes.
- Consider what new skills and knowledge will be developed and how fidelity of approach will ensure consistency of delivery.
- Do not dismiss the importance of how teachers regard the CPD and the forum in which it is delivered. Look carefully at times, days, locations and presenters.

2 Behaviour: Ideology, evidence and pragmatism

Chapter overview

From zero tolerance to restorative practice, behaviour is a divisive topic. In this chapter, I aim to acknowledge the range of different behaviour management models that exist and cut through the debates to provide actionable advice for your classroom.

Recommendations:

Featuring podcast episodes with:

- **Iggy Rhodes**, June 2019
- **Tom Bennett**, September 2020
- **Paul Dix**, June 2020

'The Smiths' B-side that never was… Some Schools Are Harder Than Others.'
Phil Naylor in conversation with Tom Bennett, September 2020

The title of this chapter is also the title of a presentation I do when asked to speak about behaviour at conferences around the country. It has taken me the best part of this 20-year career to develop a modicum of pragmatism and this is the journey of its development.

'Some schools are harder than others' (to play on Morrissey's song title *Some Girls Are Bigger Than Others*) may sound obvious, but it's a sobering epithet. When I made the move from football coaching into teaching, I like to think I was well versed in dealing with motivation, time management, resource management and even behaviour. My first school, as I've mentioned in the previous chapter, was an extremely high-performing school with relatively few behaviour issues. Under these circumstances, it is incredibly easy to be idealistic about the best way to deal with behaviour. I know this from first-hand experience. I would listen to the trials and tribulations of my peers at conferences for new teachers and wonder why they just didn't use the simple and obvious methods that we had in my school. Some of these methods could be best described using the outdated but evergreen phrase 'firm but fair'.

Ideology is rife in education for better or worse. It is important to have a philosophy, an ethos, with some guiding principles upon which to work. When this spills over into evangelising, it can create problems. Fortunately, early in my career we were not subject to the circuitous and binary behaviour discussions on social media. I'm rather ashamed to admit that I did believe there was a best way to deal with behaviour, which was based on my narrow lens in what I later discovered is a complex world.

When delivering my presentation about behaviour, I start off by asking the audience to summarise the different approaches to behaviour that they have either directly experienced, read about or seen implemented in their schools. Below is a non-exhaustive and non-judgemental list of a selection of the prevailing ideologies with regard to behaviour:

- warm strict
- zero tolerance
- no excuses
- evidence-based or research-based
- assertive discipline
- traditional
- child-centred
- common sense
- ban the booths
- firm but fair
- restorative.

As mentioned, the first school I worked in had relatively few behaviour issues. The school had a fine tradition of exemplary conduct backed up by a simple behaviour policy. Its ideology was firm but fair, with a smattering of restorative practice. The in-class behaviour system was relatively straightforward. It was a simple process of: informal warning, formal warning, name on the board, name on the board followed by a tick, and finally removal from the classroom. The names that were ticked on the board were then transferred to a sheet in the staffroom where all the teachers could see what kind of day their form group or year group were having. I can still recall the gulp from the head's PA when she delivered a list two pages long to the staffroom one fateful Friday. A Monday staff meeting was hastily called to discuss behaviour.

In those days, staff training on behaviour was minimal and this continues to be the case according to Tom Bennett as discussed on the podcast, where he argued that it is inexplicable how little time is spent in teaching teachers how to run the room:

'Behaviour management isn't particularly well trained at national and indeed at international level… Don't get me wrong, there are some great providers out there, both school-based and uni-based. But, in general, it's not very well taught. Because it's undersold in training, you tend to get this quite… I would call it an immature conversation about behaviour management.' Tom Bennett

In the first school I taught at, there was almost a reluctance to admit that any student could be capable of poor behaviour. The implication was that any conduct that was less than optimal was a result of a lack of engagement in the lessons. For this, I don't blame the school. It was the prevailing narrative nationally summarised by the urban myth of: 'Is your lesson worth behaving for?'

As many early career teachers do, I struggled with behaviour. I had particular concerns with my Year 9 class – another common issue. I plucked up the courage to seek out the deputy head to raise these concerns. The deputy was a consummate professional, immaculately turned out and an excellent teacher of many years' standing. She was ensconced in a palatial office with her own toilet (why did all leaders have separate toilets in those days – were nerves worse or was it easier for a crafty fag?). It would be fair to say that her probationary year (have a look on Google if you don't know what this is) was a dim and distant memory and when she offered advice to a new teacher from her lofty vantage point it could seem at best crass and at worst condescending. On this occasion, when I mentioned a particular Year 9 student I was finding challenging, I was met with: 'You're having problems with Charlotte? I simply can't understand that… she's so good for me.'

Quite what reaction the deputy expected to elicit from this sage piece of advice only she can explain, but it did little to help my morale and provided me with no tools to address this student's behaviours in future lessons. I naturally gravitated towards more, shall we say, 'engaging' lessons with Class 9X on a Friday afternoon. We went through a great deal of poster paper that year and I spent way too much money on chocolate bars, reward stickers and stamps. We got by and thanks to these ham-fisted attempts at trial and error my behaviour management improved incrementally. My standing, reputation and profile became enhanced. I also continued to try to teach my subject to the best of my ability and I stuck around like the Duracell Bunny, coming back lesson after lesson, week after week, maybe not quite showing unconditional positive regard but certainly showing my bright face when I didn't always feel it. Over time a relationship was built with Class 9X, and the behaviour did begin to improve.

In this chapter, I want to explore three key recommendations for effective classroom management based on my conversations with a number of experienced teachers and behaviour experts on the podcast. I hope this advice will provide you with some helpful tools, inspiration and motivation for the next time you're dealing with your very own Class 9X.

Recommendation 1: Get to know your pupils and where they are at

This recommendation is from the EEF guidance report, 'Improving behaviour in schools', as discussed with the co-author of this report Iggy Rhodes on the podcast. The precise recommendation from the EEF is: 'Know and understand your pupils and their influences'. This advice has its roots in the educational equivalent of 'Which came first, the chicken or the egg?', namely 'Which come first, relationships or rules?' Some teachers feel that it's relationships that come first and learners need to be in the correct frame of mind to be able to learn. Others feel it is important for students to first understand there are parameters to work within and that teachers are in charge of running the room. These educators feel that relationships will be born out of respect and adherence to the rules. There are of course some teachers who remain on the fence: they feel that relationships are important but it's not all about the relationships. This debate has been played out in discussions on the podcast with leading practitioners in behaviour.

The EEF guidance report on behaviour suggests that 'every pupil should have a supportive relationship with a member of school staff'. This was something discussed with Paul Dix in conversation about his book *When the Adults Change, Everything Changes* (2017). Paul talks about the concept of 'deliberate botheredness'. He suggests that teachers should go out and watch students play football, turn up at school concerts or help on Duke of Edinburgh, for example. In the book, Paul says: 'Opportunities to build emotional currency are easy to find... the trip you organise, the disco you stay late for, the door you hold.' The EEF guidance report concurs with the broad concept of botheredness when it talks about how these relationships can be achieved at the teacher's level. They suggest this could be as simple as asking about a pupil's weekend or how their football team is performing.

However, Tom Bennett sounds a cautionary note in his book *Running the Room* (2020) and suggests that although relationships are important in understanding your pupils and their influences, it's not all about relationships. In the book, he states: 'Those who claim that good behaviour is "all about relationships" need to deal with this problem: how can people behave well in communities where they have no relationship with the majority of their fellow citizens? The answer is, of course, law.'

Relationships may not be everything, but they can have a powerful impact in the classroom. Paul Dix's notion of botheredness can be employed by all educators but particularly by class teachers in primary schools and form tutors in secondary schools. These teachers are probably best placed to understand the pupil's life context and to be able to use this to inform their dealings with them. In our conversations on the podcast, Iggy Rhodes advocates that, where possible, every pupil should be known by at least one adult, who is aware of the pupil's specific background, their interests and their hobbies. However, she concedes that this is not always possible and in these contexts it's best to prioritise the pupils it's particularly difficult to build rapport with, for example, those engaging with especially challenging behaviours, those who are quiet or withdrawn, and those who aren't participating or concentrating in lessons. She recommends:

'Pick a pupil and for two minutes every day for two school weeks or ten days, talk to that pupil, not about their school work but just about themselves, and have a wider chat that's not specifically about learning. That can then help with the learning conversations that come later.' Iggy Rhodes

If I think back to the challenges I had with Charlotte in Class 9X, I recall that one day I decided to try a different tack and approached Charlotte's form tutor. It was a real eye-opener when the form tutor began to share the incredible complexity of Charlotte's home life. I had noticed, albeit subconsciously, in recent weeks

To hear more from
Iggy Rhodes, scan this
QR code.

the threadbare ends of her blazer and the flapping soles of her shoes as she breezed past me on our way into the classroom. I had been entirely focused on controlling the misbehaviour and had not allowed myself time to get to know or understand Charlotte. Following my discussion, I consciously made the effort to be more bothered and to exhibit more botheredness. I began to pay more attention to positive conduct and when Charlotte or any other students were noticeably and visibly on task, I'd praise them.

Initially, this elicited nothing more than strange looks, but over time this recognition did increase the class's adherence to classroom rules. I began to attempt positive phone calls home, the first three of which resulted in the phone being slammed down immediately as soon as I said who I was! Clearly the parents were extremely used to the school number bearing nothing but bad news. Eventually, I did get the chance to speak to Charlotte's dad and simply told him I was calling to share positive stories from today's lesson. His stunned silence and muted appreciation indicated to me that this was probably the first time this had ever happened in the ten years of schooling Charlotte had received to this point.

Did this mean that I let up on recording any other behaviours? Were any of the classroom rules not followed? No. The consistency and application of the school's behaviour policy remained, and this allowed other students to feel safe and of equal importance. My practice was developing to become more evidence-informed and more bothered. Over time, my relationship with Charlotte did begin to improve to the point that when I saw Charlotte in the school yard the year after, she lamented those Friday afternoon lessons and told me how she now enjoys science.

After my successes with Charlotte, I became more interested in the art and science of behaviour. I began to research and dig deeper into some of the more complex factors that may be affecting behaviour. Some of these factors are within the control of the classroom teacher, some are within the control of the school and others require more specialist help and intervention. These might range from adverse childhood experiences, bullying, mental health problems and other complex factors. As I discussed with Iggy, once a teacher feels in an informed position, they can build understanding about a specific pupil or situation and then in turn identify and implement the most effective behaviour management approach.

So, the conclusion to be drawn from this is that it is important to understand the pupils in front of you and their motivations and influences. The cultivation, creation and maintenance of relationships are extremely important, but this is only one factor in improving behaviour in schools.

Naylor's nuggets

- There is a strong evidence base that teacher–pupil relationships are important in good behaviour and that these relationships can directly influence a pupil's attainment and effort.
- A pragmatic approach to developing these relationships is essential: try selecting one pupil you think it would be beneficial to get to know and focus on building that relationship for two minutes every day over the course of two weeks.
- It is vital to have awareness of influences that may affect children's behaviour, including adverse childhood experiences, bullying, mental health and other complex factors. Seek specialist help in meeting the needs of these children if required.

Recommendation 2: Actively teach behaviour alongside addressing misbehaviour

'The successful management of behaviour relies on far more than a set of strategies to draw upon when pupils misbehave.' Ellis and Tod (2018)

The aforementioned deputy head (you remember… the one with the toilet) also suggested as part of her advice on behaviour management that I should go and observe experienced teachers teaching their classes. At least this piece of advice was said with my best interests at heart and was a genuine attempt to develop my craft. The problem with this was that many of the teachers had been at the school since the late 1970s. Consequently, they had total credibility and unimpeachable reputations. They had taught generation after generation of the same families so that many of the techniques and skills they deployed to produce an educational oasis of calm were implicit rather than explicit. I vividly remember enjoying an art lesson where the teacher (chain smoking in the lesson!) was listening to sixties psychedelia whilst modelling and demonstrating how to draw a portrait. Even with my naiveties, I noticed that none of the observations the deputy head had suggested involved watching Charlotte in another teacher's lesson. I did think at the time this was quite deliberate.

The online retailer Amazon opened its virtual doors in the early 2000s and with it came a treasure trove of professional development, which was sadly lacking in education before those years. I dived in at the deep end, purchasing anything and everything to do with behaviour. In my library at home, I have some absolute gems of that era, including *Brain Gym* (Dennison and Dennison, 1989), *Super Teaching* (Jensen, 2008) and any number of books advocating active learning methods and promoting engagement rather than knowledge. One book did stand out and, to a certain extent, stood the test of time. The book in question is *Assertive Discipline* by Lee Canter (2009). This was a book I devoured in one sitting during the summer holidays of 2003 and continued to go back to at the beginning of every academic year for the next decade. What this book brought out and explained clearly was that behaviour management required more than managing misbehaviour; it actually needed to help teach students how to behave. Iggy discussed this when talking through the EEF's guidance report on the podcast and cited that the climate for learning can be improved through the teaching of these learning behaviours, which in turn reduces the time needed to be constantly managing misbehaviour.

Contrary to the binary debates happening on social media, there seems to be a great deal of consensus on this point. The EEF guidance report (2019b) discussed with Iggy, *Running the Room* (2020) discussed with Tom Bennett, and *When the Adults Change, Everything Changes* (2017) discussed with Paul Dix all broadly agree that there are two approaches to behaviour management, both importantly underpinned by long-term detailed implementation. These are a proactive approach (getting in front of behaviour and planning for behaviour) and a reactive approach (dealing with behaviour when it has happened). Let's have a look at what we mean by proactive, reactive and implementation in this context.

Proactive: The classroom environment is created for both the adults and the children. Where both parties understand the expectations in the classroom, there are good relationships with emotionally consistent adults. Proactive strategies seek to reduce the chances of any poor behaviour occurring.

Reactive: This involves simply responding to pupils' behaviour as and when it happens. This also encompasses what happens following the behaviour and supporting students to improve their behaviour in future.

Implementation: This is the execution of a plan or idea. Implementation is so important and pivotal to your approach that it is explored further in Recommendation 3 on page 49.

Successful behaviour management involves a healthy combination of both proactive and reactive approaches. While the reactive strategies available to a teacher are often guided by their school's behaviour policy (whether that's formal or informal warnings, sanctions or restorative practices), proactive approaches can be more nuanced and individualised. So how can teachers go about being more proactive with their behaviour management?

Being more proactive

As my career has progressed, I have been privileged to work with new entrants to the profession as a professional mentor. When working closely with ECTs, I have noticed they are often surprised at how well the new class behaves during their first lesson. Having observed these classes for a number of weeks prior to taking control, it can come as a little bit of a surprise to see how engaged the previously apathetic Year 3 class are for a new teacher. ECTs may reflect that their captivating content has inspired the class and proceed to spend endless energetic hours planning for the subsequent lessons.

Without fail, on a rainy Tuesday afternoon the honeymoon period ends abruptly. They just can't understand what has changed and how the lesson could have been so different to the ones they'd taught before. It may be controversial, but a view I discussed with Tom Bennett on the podcast is that there is not enough time spent on the art and science of behaviour during the period of initial teacher training. New teachers (and teachers who are new to a school) often spend hours preparing for the curriculum and the teaching and learning aspect of their role and very little time preparing for any potential misbehaviour. Tom Bennett, in our discussions on the podcast, explains how this then transfers to classroom practice:

 'One of the big mistakes that a lot of teachers make when they enter a classroom is they won't teach the behaviour that they expect. They'll simply try to teach the subject that they are there to teach, whether that be mathematics or PE or music. They'll look at the class, and the class will look at them, and they'll say, "Right. Hello, it's a pleasure to meet you. My name is Mr Bennett. Let's now do the kings of England (or something)."' Tom Bennett

So how can teachers be more prepared for behaviour management? Chapter 1 looks at the importance of professional development and this is pertinent again here. Take time to read books, attend training courses, listen to podcasts and engage in conversations about behaviour. Whether you feel that your teacher training on behaviour was sufficient or not, there is always more to learn.

I alluded earlier to my use of educational books for my own professional development, including Lee Canter's *Assertive Discipline* (2009). One of Lee's suggestions, which was quite revolutionary at the time, was the need to set out expectations and rules in the first few lessons and continue to teach behaviour throughout the academic year. Lee argued, 'The number one priority for teachers at the beginning of the year is not teaching the three R's but rather systematically teaching students the appropriate behaviours needed to be successful in classroom activities.' At the time this did seem reasonably controversial as there was (and to a lesser extent still is) a prevailing notion in schools and particularly at secondary level that: 'Pupils should know how to behave by now.'

Since the publication of *Assertive Discipline*, the 'rules lesson' has become a regular feature in the early days of September each year, as teachers set out their stall early on and pupils are clear about the expectations for the full year. Paul Dix, in his book *After the Adults Change* (2021), acknowledges the need to teach behaviour but questions the need for a rules lesson:

> 'Consistency cannot be established in a single lesson any more than how to behave can be taught in a single lesson. Your students need high expectations, tight routines and essential rules drip-fed over time. Delivering it all at once is as realistic as delivering the entire science curriculum in a double lesson.'

Being proactive can be summarised as 'teaching pupils the way that we do things around here'. This will be in large part dictated by the culture of the school, but a teacher is able to control their own environment to a certain extent and define what is normal in their classroom. Whilst the rules lesson can be useful to define norms, these have to be explicitly taught over time and acknowledged and reinforced constantly.

Proactive therefore also means constantly teaching the behaviours you want to see. This can be applied to classroom teachers of any level of experience or seniority. At the time of recording my interview with Paul Dix, I had recently been appointed as deputy headteacher leading on behaviour in a new school at Christmas time. I discussed with Paul how I had expected that when I sailed into my Year 11 classroom, the students would be stunned into respectful silence by the mere mention of the words 'deputy head'. I had expected that my metaphorical cape trailing behind me and superhero badge on my suit would be enough for the class to settle into what was expected. I experienced the same 'honeymoon period' as the ECTs I mentioned earlier. The headteacher would come into my lessons and remark on how well-behaved and engaged students appeared to be. I had, however, made the fundamental mistake of assumption. I hadn't taught the rules lesson! As it was midway through the academic year, and I was operating with a very clear and well-explained behaviour policy that was displayed and summarised in a one-pager on the wall, I just assumed that I could stand up and teach rates of chemical reaction without any issues. After two weeks of this honeymoon period, things started to slide. Students drifted in later and later, coats started to appear on students' backs and bags were now on desks with phones propped up behind them. My conversation with Paul illustrated that behaviour management is not something to be achieved; it's something that needs constant work.

In our conversation we looked at one of Paul's ideas in his first book, *When the Adults Change, Everything Changes* (2017):

> *'Catching them being good is not enough. If you want to dramatically shift the standard of behaviour of your students, then catch them when they are behaving over and above and mark it with positive recognition.'*

Rather than coming into the classroom immediately looking for misbehaviour and setting out to correct it, Paul and I considered ways to become more proactive to reinforce the positive behaviour that the majority were exhibiting and to teach the other students some learning behaviours. In my practice, by first paying attention to the best conduct, my mindset was slightly altered and I was able to be calmer and more consistent and focused on delivering for the students.

With Tom Bennett, I also discussed the theme of establishing norms, which are the embodiment of the way that things are done in any establishment. These norms really help all teachers to be proactive, as they should be understood and applied by everyone. There are undoubted benefits to the establishment and maintenance of norms, but there is not universal agreement on their need or use. In Tom's words:

> *'The weird thing I find about people who object to systematising behaviour in the classroom is they think that it somehow roboticises children. People often say, "You're a monster, Bennett. You don't want children to think." You know*

what? I don't! I don't want children to think about where their pens are. I don't want them to have to think about how to sit. I don't want them to have to think about where their jacket goes. I want that to be utterly subliminal. I want that to be done unconsciously. I want to free up their working memories so that they can think about art and music and poetry and science and every other wonderful, magical thing that learning can offer them.' Tom Bennett

At the time of recording with Tom, schools were preparing to go back in September 2020, following the long, enforced partial school closures due to the COVID-19 pandemic. Tom and I discussed how to get in front of behaviour, which was a concern for myself and for listeners as we returned to our classrooms. Tom also acknowledged the importance of teaching learning behaviours through establishing norms. Tom uses a particular model to help with this, which he calls the 'know, teach and maintain model'. I discussed a particular rule from my school, namely coats not being allowed on inside the building, with Tom. Here is how this rule could be achieved using Tom's model:

To hear more from **Tom Bennett**, scan this QR code.

Know: It is important for students and staff to understand why this particular rule is in place. It could be that the uniform is intended to engender a sense of pride and belonging, which is obscured by the coat. It could be that to safeguard students, staff have to be sure that all students can be identified by their uniform. Helping to explain the rule via assemblies will create buy-in and co-operation.

Teach: This could be as simple as thanking students for taking off their jackets as they enter the building. It could be a quick 30-second conversation to remind a recalcitrant student on a Monday morning and the absolute surety of follow-through for students not adhering to the rule. This again strengthens the culture of 'the way we do things around here' and makes things easier for all staff.

Maintain: We have all experienced the annual uniform crackdown during the first days and weeks of September, in which the headteacher or senior leaders declare this is the year when uniform will be sorted. In our case, all coats will be off in the building. However, once lessons start in earnest and the busyness of everyday school life takes over, the teaching of learning behaviours seems to dissipate.

Maintenance and consistency are hugely important, and this starts from the top. If the headteacher doesn't enforce this, it becomes harder for all teachers to do so.

Naylor's nuggets

- Teach learning behaviours. Being proactive in your approach to get in front of behaviour will reduce the need to be reactive and manage misbehaviour. There will always be a need for both proactive and reactive strategies and approaches.
- Calm and consistent classroom management can reduce challenging behaviours and improve pupil disengagement.
- Effective implementation with consistent approaches is vital for the success of any classroom management strategy.

Recommendation 3: Consistency is crucial

In the last part of Tom's 'know, teach and maintain model' demonstrated on page 48, he talks about the importance of maintaining learning behaviours, which leads us nicely into this next section on consistency and implementation. An area of near full agreement between all the behaviour experts spoken to on the podcast is the need for consistency of application of your behaviour policy.

Let's take a minute to remind ourselves of Chapter 1 on continuing professional development and the story shared by Dr Thomas Guskey of his dread that his headteacher would go on a training course and then come back with great ideas that would need to be implemented (page 15). Whilst behaviour management training does not take place often enough, when it does there seems to be a need to jump straight from the page of the training manual to practice in the classroom. Behaviour is notoriously difficult to change quickly, and small, incremental, day-in-day-out efforts pay dividends in the long run.

Let's start first with adults' behaviour. This is an extremely thorny issue as teachers are of course professionals and behave in a professional manner at all times. However, teachers are also human beings, and our behaviour is influenced by internal and external factors and the incredibly demanding nature of the day-to-day job.

Tom Bennett in *Running the Room* (2020) says that:

'The culture of your classroom isn't a thing separate from you. It is made up of you, your actions, your expectations, and what you permit or prohibit.'

Paul Dix explores this same theme more thoroughly in his book *When the Adults Change, Everything Changes* (2017). He talks in detail about the consistency of adult behaviours and the constancy of adults' emotions. He explains the importance of this in the context of children's lives and how in some cases, school is the only place where they receive consistency and surety in adult behaviour:

'The solid base of any classroom is the sure-footedness of the adults. Their certainty quells anxiety from children and creates a safe atmosphere where great learning thrives.'

To hear more from **Paul Dix**, scan this QR code.

So, what does the evidence say about consistency? In the EEF (2019b) guidance report on behaviour, consistency is a recommendation all of its own (Recommendation 6), which carries across all five other recommendations. The guidance says that consistency and coherence at a whole-school level are paramount. Before we get into whole-school recommendations, however, let's look at what individual teachers can do in their classrooms. Recommendation 4 from the EEF report is:

'Use simple approaches as part of your regular routine.'

It is entirely understandable that consistency is difficult to achieve, particularly in what have been extremely challenging times. There are also the incredible internal and external pressures on teachers, not least the intervention merry-go-round and constant scrutiny from politicians and Ofsted. A quick-fix culture around behaviour has led to many approaches that the evidence in the EEF report suggests may be less than helpful, for example zero tolerance.

What do we mean by routines?

So, there seems to be a great deal of talk about routine and the importance of consistency. Therefore, in this section we will look at what we mean by routines. We will ask whether there are particular routines that are desirable in schools. We will look at what people had to say about routines in our podcast episodes and in their books, and we will give you some examples. We will also consider whether it's important to teach routines and we will then finish by examining the benefits of routines.

In my conversations with Tom Bennett on the podcast, Tom talks about the importance of routines:

 'Routines are an essential part of the schoolteacher's apparatus when it comes to creating a culture. I mean, I'm reaching here slightly, but a routine is basically a norm, in the sense that it's a set sequence of behaviours that you expect to be done pretty much without exception, pretty much all the time.' **Tom Bennett**

Paul Dix is also aware of the importance of routines and how some routines are essential to the everyday running of the classroom; he calls these 'keystone' routines. If we get into some examples from *When the Adults Change, Everything Changes* (2017), Paul talks about the 'keystones' and they are as follows:

- getting the class silent and ready for instruction
- setting the class to work
- reflective questioning
- educating or even eliciting success criteria.

Tom Bennett also talks about different routines. He devotes a whole chapter of *Running the Room* (2020) to discussing many different types of routines. This includes social and academic routines to be used in the classroom, and social routines to be used around the rest of the school at times of transitions (such as lunchtimes and breaktimes). A common theme is that there should be a small number of routines that are understood by all. When I spoke with Tom in the summer of 2020, I was very keen to learn how I could devise some routines to be used both to improve behaviour and be proactive in our response to the pandemic and the regulations schools had to operate under. Tom suggested his 5 D's model from *Running the Room*:

1. Design: Think about the routines you want and need.
2. Describe: Ensure the students know the routines you have chosen.
3. Demonstrate: Demonstrate the routines to students so they know what they look like in practice.
4. Demand: Reinforce the routines as 'the way we do things around here'.
5. Disengage: Take a step back and evaluate the routines: do they now run without constant reinforcement and micromanagement?

Routines: an example

In an afternoon of great inspiration (these are few and far between...), I came up with the following routines that may be useful to the reader as the exemplification of the 5 D's model and that you may potentially want to use in your school.

DESIGN
Academic and social routines:

1. On time to shine
2. Dress to impress
3. Collect and inspect
4. Left is best
5. South Shore Star
6. Hands up, hush up
7. Stand and deliver

DESCRIBE

1. **On time to shine:** This is a routine to help us throughout our lives. As a community we are on time and ready to start by the allotted time. Being on time ensures school and lessons can start on time. In the period of COVID-19, it also reduces chances of bubble mixing and disease transmission.

2. **Dress to impress:** We believe that our uniform represents us as a community. We are proud to belong to the community of South Shore Academy. We ensure that our uniform is correct every day. This includes our PE kit.

3. **Collect and inspect:** Teachers will arrive to the allotted space or classroom and collect students. They will inspect uniform and note any absences or other issues. Staff and students will greet each other.

4. **Left is best:** To ensure a smooth and safe transition around the building, we walk on the left as guided by the arrows on the corridors and staircases.

5. **South Shore Star:** We sit up, track the speaker, ask and answer questions, and respect each other and our building.

6. **Hands up, hush up:** When any member of staff raises their hand, we all raise our hands and are silent.

7. **Stand and deliver:** At the end of the lesson, students will stand and will be delivered to their next destination. Students will thank the teacher.

DEMONSTRATE

The nature of many of the routines listed here meant that they were public and visible, with many opportunities for demonstration. Heads of year were involved in demonstrating how this would look in the first instances. They could encourage and, if necessary, challenge staff to make sure that they were correctly collecting their students. This public setting also encouraged a real team approach and ethic.

If we look at the third of these routines, namely 'Collect and inspect', this is not a routine that can be practised live due to the potential for confusion. To mitigate this, I shot a video in the sunny summer afternoons using my own children. We videoed them lining up outside on the markers and being collected by the teacher (me) and inspected for their uniform in order to model and demonstrate the whole process. The video was then skilfully edited and shared with all staff ahead of INSET days and again during those sessions. The video was also explained to all pupils by their form tutors during the first days back.

DEMAND

The early days and weeks went smoothly thanks to the demonstrations. The challenge was to prevent the slide that normally happens following the introduction of a new routine. Think how many times you've joined a gym and given up in February; think how many times you've heard at a September INSET that 'this is the year we will sort out behaviour'.

To help with the demand phase, we ensured that all senior leaders and middle leaders were outside during every change. If we weren't supervising our own classes, we would be at the doors to support the staff. This collectivism reinforces the way we do things around here. It is important for staff and students to see that senior staff are reinforcing key routines and living them through both words and actions. There is of course some overlap here, so positive reinforcement and positive correction were also used but, where needed, the possibility of sanction was present.

DISENGAGE

We had a consultant who would come into school periodically to look at our behaviour policy and its application. He was extremely complimentary about our new routines and commented on how hard the leadership team were working to enforce them. He unknowingly coined a phrase that hopefully helps explain the disengage section:

'What would happen if you had a tea and biscuits moment?'

What he meant by this is: would the routines still run if they were not being constantly reinforced and micromanaged? When those early weeks have passed and the routines are now becoming embedded, is it possible to step back and see if they just run? This will also allow everyone to step up and own the routines, further fostering that sense of the way we do things here. It also future-proofs key roles; especially during the pandemic, with high levels of absence, it has made cover much easier, even for key roles, as everyone knows how to work within routines. Routines also help to settle students. Finally, the disengage stage helps leaders to take stock and evaluate what is going well and what needs to change, something that is harder to do when they are in the thick of the day-to-day.

Naylor's nuggets

- Consistency underpins everything with regard to behaviour policy and practice.
- Be mindful of implementation and consider the need for routines. Think about the type of routines required in your setting, referring to the examples of routines provided here. Also consider how many routines to introduce at a particular time.
- Look at communicating and teaching your routines in the same way as for a curriculum. Behaviour needs to be taught and reinforced like a curriculum.

3 Leadership lessons

Chapter overview

This chapter will draw out key themes from our podcast conversations about leadership. From leading pupils in your classroom to being a head of department or even leading a whole school, the recommendations in this chapter will support you in prioritising, strategising and developing expertise.

Recommendations:

Featuring podcast episodes with:

- **Matthew Evans**, January 2020
- **Drew Povey**, December 2020
- **Professor Becky Allen**, November 2021
- **Tom Rees**, January 2021
- **Dr Jill Berry**, October 2019
- **Neil Reynolds**, August 2020
- **Professor Michael Young**, August 2019
- **Aziza Ajak**, July 2020

This has undoubtedly been the chapter that has evolved the most over time. At the start of the podcast, in those early months of 2019, we had some clear ideas of what leadership in education looked like. We also had plenty of literature on leadership styles and what type of leader teachers may aspire to be. What has been significant and noticeable in the duration of the podcast so far is how this has changed seismically both due to the political climate and due to the COVID-19 pandemic.

These events have shifted the dial on what it means to be a leader of an education establishment and the conversations on the podcast have reflected that. Listening to the episodes chronologically, as I have in the preparation of this book, it has been fascinating to document the changing environment in which leaders have had to operate. From the Blitz spirit of the early months, with the heroic stories of sacrifice and selfless community service, to last-minute adaptations during partial closures and the day-to-day existence of the 'pingdemic', where teachers and leaders had to self-isolate at the ping of an app. Leaders have had to be extraordinarily adaptable, pragmatic and stoic. Some of the characteristics that would have headlined any writing on leadership pre-pandemic, such as vision and strategy, have receded temporarily while leaders wrestle with the everyday, not always knowing what is around the corner.

This chapter is not designed to be a catch-all guide to leadership, but a snapshot of the characteristics and traits that have been deployed by leaders navigating their way through one of the most challenging periods in recent history. In reading their thoughts and accessing their interviews, some of the best lessons from leading in challenging times will come through.

Leadership exists at all levels in any organisation, but this is especially true of teaching. By design, you are the leader of the class you are teaching, and your behaviour is scrutinised, copied and even emulated by those in your charge. There are also many and varied trajectories and directions you can go in as a leader. There are teachers who would like to stay in the classroom, leading by example in their pedagogy and practice. There are other teachers who would like to take on responsibilities outside the classroom, leading the next generation of teachers or improving the current crop through coaching and mentoring. Some teachers who have a real passion for their subject or discipline look to lead departments and faculties. Middle leadership can also focus on responsibilities for a particular year group, key stage or whole-school priority area, such as behaviour. Senior leadership roles can be many and varied; they can be classroom-based, operational or strategic. In recent years, an extra layer of system leadership has also developed, which involves working across schools and academy trusts in a role that is less pupil facing but no less crucial.

There is no one definition of leadership in a holistic school sense that can be easily understood, applied and assimilated by the whole profession. As discussed with Tom Rees, the author of many books on leadership, on the podcast:

'It means different things to different people; it lacks a clear definition.'
Tom Rees

Herein lies a significant challenge with school leadership: without a clear definition, how do you know what best practice looks like in leadership and how do you know if what you're doing is working? As headteacher and author Matthew Evans says:

'If you don't have a definition of something, you can't test it. So, what I found increasingly was that the ideas about leadership were very much dependent on the perspective you took on leadership.' Matthew Evans

In this chapter, sticking with the narrative and purpose of the book, we will look to learn lessons and take themes from what has been discussed in regard to school leadership with our 130 podcast guests. I have spent hours diligently assimilating and transcribing all our interviews and I have finally settled on six key themes that come through our discussions. You will find them presented below, along with practical guidance and ideas, as well as my handy 'Naylor's nuggets' summaries.

Recommendation 1: Take charge

In research that has been published over the last 20 to 30 years, the word 'leadership' has become popular and in education it has taken over in the main from 'management'. Senior teams have moved from being 'senior management teams (SMT)' to 'senior leadership teams (SLT)'. Management is a term that now has negative connotations, indicating prescriptive control over people and situations, which can be seen as oppressive. Leadership in all its myriad different forms has become the most talked about topic on our podcast. Generic leadership skills such as strong leadership, charismatic leadership and dynamic leadership have often been the topics of discussion, but what do they mean and are they still relevant in times of huge change?

Speaking with Matthew Evans on the podcast in January 2020, we agreed that these generic leadership skills exist in isolation, are not domain specific and therefore serve as a false set of expertise. In fact, leadership is highly dependent on context. The knowledge and skills needed to lead a school are developed by experiences in very specific circumstances. Matthew made the pitfalls of this clear:

'[You undervalue] actually understanding your context and the specific things that make your school what it is. If you don't value that context, you stop enquiring, you stop talking to people and you stop finding out more. You become quite fixed in your view of yourself as a leader, that you are good at what you do and there's not much more to learn.' Matthew Evans

To hear more from
Matthew Evans, scan this
QR code.

As the pandemic took hold in early 2020, these conversations echoed in my mind. My own personal circumstance at this historic juncture was that I was at the very start of a deputy headship. I had, through my application and interview, formulated and reflected on the leadership styles that would best suit me when beginning in a new school mid-year. I planned to be pragmatic and establish the lie of the land, keeping the best of what was already working, making tweaks to systems and structures, and working collaboratively with teachers and leaders. Within weeks, my best-laid plans and visions were parked to begin planning for partial closures and lockdowns. In this context, I had to 'take charge'.

In times of crisis and great change, management can precede and eventually supplement leadership. A notable example from history is the famous pairing of Winston Churchill and Clement Attlee as Prime Minister and Deputy Prime Minister, respectively, during the Second World War. Churchill's vision of 'no surrender' would have been empty and useless without Attlee's meticulous planning and methodical operations. Taking charge does not necessarily mean shouting and haranguing but it does mean being prepared to make decisions.

Leaders in 2020, 2021, 2022 and beyond have had to make many decisions, many of which they had not been expecting or had any training in how to do. They have had to steer schools through partial closures, create testing centres, manage bubbles, support the most vulnerable in society through free school meals vouchers and continue to ensure students are safe, learning and achieving. This could not have been done through visionary leadership, as nobody's vision would have foreseen what was on the horizon in March 2020 and nobody's vision can see what will be coming next.

A quite distinctive style of leadership has therefore evolved. Taking charge has shaken off any negative connotations and has become a necessity for school leaders. All stakeholders need to know where to look when times are challenging; school leaders in 2021 have embodied clarity of decisions and sureness of purpose. The domain-specific knowledge and skills discussed with Matthew in early 2020 will become relevant once more as we navigate a return to the normal, but behind these skills and competencies sits a vital lesson: 'When the going gets tough, the tough get going' (Billy Ocean).

Naylor's nuggets

- In times of crisis and change, be prepared to take charge: you may have long-term plans and ambitious visions for your school but sometimes these need to be parked in order to deal with the here and now.
- Avoid complacency: remember that leadership is not one-size-fits-all. You need to develop skills, expertise and leadership styles that are specific to the context you are working within and what is happening around you.
- Quick decision-making, meticulous planning and methodical operations often win the day.

Recommendation 2: Know what you want to do

When I was in the process of applying for deputy head positions, I was fortunate to have the opportunity to speak with many great leaders on the podcast. Their advice is woven through this chapter. I was also extremely lucky to have had the ear of former headteachers and senior leaders whom I have worked with over my career. I'd arrive to meet with them at various coffee shops and houses across the north-west, usually armed with my CV, letters of application and a list of my 'accomplishments to date'. Even in retirement, the leaders were still extremely sharp and astute, capable of reducing me to a stuttering wreck. This is particularly true of the opening question each of them posed to me:

'Why do you want to be a deputy head?'

Before I was able to muster an attempt at an answer, I was quickly sitting back to drink from the fountain of experience. My former headteacher shared a story from her experience when an assistant headteacher on interview for deputy headship had struggled with this question. The assistant head simply said that he felt that, due to his experience, it was the next step for him and he deserved the chance to be deputy headteacher. Needless to say, he didn't make it on that occasion, but it does illustrate the wider point here. Many leaders apply for a job or a position as they think this is their next step, the next promotion, or because they feel that they can do the job. If this well-intentioned but misguided leader achieves their dream promotion, what will life under their leadership look like? Unfortunately, we have all worked for these leaders. The lack of purpose and direction means that the organisation can be buffeted by the winds of change, blown off course by every new idea and gimmick in education and finally derailed by the everyday crises and issues that come to define a directionless tenure.

It is vital that an aspiring leader has an obvious reason and rationale for applying for the job. The leader must come in with a vision for what they want to achieve and a plan for its execution. They should also understand why the staff want to work at the school, why the parents send their children to the school and what can be achieved for their students. As I've mentioned, the single best piece of research in this area is the EEF's 'Guide to implementation' (2019a). This details a process leaders can go through from identifying an issue through to its ultimate resolution. This research and further reading on leadership was summarised succinctly on the podcast with Drew Povey:

 'I think it's about understanding what they're trying to do, how they're trying to do it, and probably in the words of Simon Sinek, why they're trying to do that thing.' **Drew Povey**

Finding or discovering your why is vital to leadership, but once you've found it make sure you can keep working towards it without being frustrated at every turn. The issue here can be the disconnect between the imagined school in the leader's head and the reality that they find when they arrive in post.

'People get uncomfortable when their naive or imagined view of how the system works clashes with reality. Take the example of senior leaders who come in and they design sleek systems which they believe will be followed by all and deliver greater efficiency… only to discover that the old imperfect system works.'
Professor Becky Allen

To hear more from **Drew Povey**, scan this QR code.

This does not mean that action should not be taken towards the ambitious vision that you have for the school. It does, however, mean that in leadership, pragmatism is an important quality borne often from painful experience. If you are a new senior leader taking over in a school within a particular Ofsted category and your principal responsibilities are measurable, such as attendance or behaviour, it can be tempting to look to make substantial changes early on. But knowing what you want to do does not mean making huge

To hear more from **Professor Becky Allen,** scan this QR code.

changes from day one. In discussions with guests and from my own experience, leaders and teachers already working within challenging contexts are quite often the most knowledgeable about what works for them and have also seen many leaders come and go in short periods having made huge, unsustainable changes. Systemic changes and policy directions can often accommodate what is currently working well and the aim should be to blend that with some external expertise. These slower changes that focus on tweaking old imperfect systems gradually, with a sharp vision of what is coming down the line, can be the difference for schools that have historically struggled and existed within a quick-fix culture. Knowing what you want to do also means embracing the positives from the previous incumbent of your position.

'You're so much better than last night's audience.' Bruce Forsyth

It can be easy when starting a new position to reflect negatively on what has gone before to provide you with ground-zero for your leadership. This, of course, is pertinent and prescient in some schools where this quite literally has been the case. However, in other schools, particularly good and outstanding schools with the results to back up the judgements, this can be a problem. Talking in positive terms about some of what has gone before is accurate, respectful and motivational for teachers and staff who have worked extremely hard in that regime for that person. Ripping everything up and starting again can be necessary and is often tempting, but it is not always the best idea.

Naylor's nuggets

- When you apply for a leadership position, make sure you have a clear idea of your purpose and direction: what is the vision you want to achieve during your tenure and what is your plan for its execution?
- Be clear about the true context of the school. Do your research so you understand why staff want to work at the school, why parents send their children to the school and what can be achieved for the students.
- Don't be tempted to overhaul everything overnight. Gradual tweaks often lead to more sustainable and impactful changes.
- Draw on the expertise of those leaders and teachers who are already working at the school. Accommodate what is already working well in your long-term plans.
- Have a plan, be flexible and pragmatic, but don't get distracted.

Recommendation 3: Do not get bogged down, but close circles

In the words of Stephen Covey (2020), who of course has been a huge influence on many of the leaders interviewed here, 'It is so easy to get caught up in the thick of thin things.' This particular tip is especially pertinent for those new to post. When you are appointed to a middle or senior leadership position, it is important to be seen to be getting things done. It is also important to be available and visible to students and staff. This has its advantages in raising your profile, building rapport and giving you the satisfaction that you are busy.

Leadership roles can be strategic or operational, but in reality they are a complex mixture of both. It is much easier to be operational as all teachers are experts at dealing with the breakneck daily pace of school life and problem-solving, even firefighting, on a daily basis. It is, however, incredibly easy to become stuck in the everyday. There will often be an inbox full of emails, a queue of people at your classroom or office door and a phone that never stops ringing. In conversations on the podcast, we can see how this can become the default setting for some leaders. They willingly or unwittingly fall into the trap of the 'superhero' leader, the go-to person, the one everyone can rely on to sort everything out for them. On the podcast, Tom Rees discussed this 'hero paradigm':

 'We set leaders up as these kind of transformational, charismatic people who will transform a community and of course leaders, like teachers, are human. And so this can be problematic, and it can put people off the role, and it can create sort of false expectations of what's possible.' Tom Rees

To hear more from **Tom Rees**, scan this QR code.

In another podcast, Dr Jill Berry talked similarly about the fallibility of leaders:

 'But I think you also have to take responsibility and accept that people don't expect their leaders to be infallible.' Dr Jill Berry

The problem with being the go-to leader, the solution to everyone's problems, is that you quickly become overloaded. Rather than leading, you are now supporting. Put too much weight on a supporting beam and it will weaken, splinter and eventually break.

To hear more from **Dr Jill Berry**, scan this QR code.

This may seem dramatic, and I am not for a minute suggesting that these routine day-to-day tasks will break the senior leader, but being stuck in 'the thick of thin things' means that sometimes things are missed. Being a leader should not, and does not, mean doing everything yourself. The skills of delegation and line management are important to learn, particularly for the superhero leader.

Have you ever noticed that superheroes only rid the world of baddies for a set amount of time? They do not make plans to prevent the creation and propagation of the next generations of baddies. They simply swoop in, solve the problem, and wait for it to happen again. Being stuck in the everyday means that the leader is not being strategic, developing staff, processes and procedures. And, extending the superhero metaphor until it is wafer thin, what happens if the superhero disappears, is killed or loses their powers? A big hole is left and people are looking at themselves to see what is next. In leadership in 2022, we should be invested in futureproofing, in making sure we have systems, structures and organisations that are less dependent on the efforts and attributes of one particular person. Quite often when the superhero leaves the school, there is a period of huge readjustment, but when a leader who is not bogged down in the everyday leaves, the school continues to run and their legacy is the smooth, efficient school they have left behind for pupils and staff.

The superhero leader can be an attractive option for senior leaders for this very reason. We all want to feel valued and we all want to be missed when we are gone. A pragmatic, strategic leader who puts systems and structures in place and quietly co-ordinates behind the scenes is not obviously noticed or recognised by staff and students, particularly in the everyday nature of schools. Politically this can be difficult for senior leaders, as unrecognised work can lead to questions about effectiveness, value for money and status within school. The anti-hero leader may, for example, be a deputy headteacher functioning extremely efficiently behind a superhero headteacher who leaves gaps for their pragmatist deputy to fill in behind the scenes. The anti-hero may work well with the charismatic leader, Penfold to their Danger Mouse, both knowing and understanding their roles in this double act. The problem can come when the anti-hero must work with a new leader who is lacking in confidence and parasitically siphons the best of the ideas to present as their own whilst publicly seeking to undermine and side-line those around them. We will come to more advice around navigating the politics of team-building and the importance of selecting the right team later in the chapter.

Even though the superhero paradigm can be appealing to some confident and charismatic teachers and leaders, this can be very off-putting for others aspiring to headship. As Tom Rees rightly identifies in the quote on page 63, in thinking that being a headteacher requires the mentality and persona of a superhero, some may be put off from applying for the role. As a leader myself, I realise that I am far from a superhero; I lack charisma and struggle to achieve the rapport that some leaders do with their staff. Nevertheless, what I do bring in vision, efficiency, implementation and consistency are also hugely important, if unadvertised, traits for a successful headteacher. These traits are also paramount for 'closing circles', which is a key aspect of effective leadership.

The 'close circles' phrase comes from podcast guest, former headteacher and manager of FC United of Manchester, Neil Reynolds. An archetypal superhero leader when viewed from the outside with his larger-than-life personality and excellent communication skills, Neil is a fascinating combination of the leadership styles discussed in this section. His attention to detail and forensic approach to tasks mark him out as the example here. Neil is rarely bogged down and not often stuck in the thick of thin things, but if a task needs doing it will be done. By 'closing circles', Neil means that if you begin a task, you should see that task through to its conclusion.

 'Never leave begun tasks incomplete. Always close circles.' Neil Reynolds

This 'closing circles' moniker, which Neil carries with him until this day, serves as an important reminder that leaders cannot spend all day in blue-sky visionary thinking, neither should they be stuck in the hamster wheel of everyday decision-making; but should leaders start a task or project they must see it through until the end. This builds confidence, credibility and provides a fitting example for teachers and pupils alike.

To hear more from **Neil Reynolds**, scan this QR code.

Naylor's nuggets

- As a leader, avoid getting bogged down in too much day-to-day administration and crisis management. Your focus should be on the big picture, so learn and practise the skills of delegation and effective line management to ensure that detailed tasks are completed with limited input from you.

- If you're hiring for a leadership role, don't overplay the importance of charisma and confidence; give equal value to vision, efficiency, implementation and consistency.
- Always close circles: if you start a task, make sure you see it through to its natural conclusion.

Recommendation 4: Develop expertise

It can sometimes seem as if a leader needs to be the proverbial jack of all trades and master of none, having the ability to wear different hats as and when the occasion or situation demands it. The last five years have seen a marked shift in the perception and expectations of teachers and leaders. In 2019, I interviewed titan of education Professor Michael Young, co-author of the seminal book *Knowledge and the Future School* (2014), for the podcast and I posed the idea of teachers and leaders becoming re-professionalised. Teachers are professionals, but the focus of previous governments on pedagogy over knowledge has meant that teachers have been seen as facilitators rather than expert professionals. The current focus on knowledge and subject specialisation will help to re-professionalise teachers.

In this context, leaders now must be at the forefront of educational research and its implications for the classroom. Leaders might have followed a pastoral or academic route into leadership, which is where their skill set may lie. However, the challenge of modern leadership is that a leader must have a working knowledge of all curriculum areas, personal development, welfare, behaviour and safeguarding, whilst retaining overall responsibility for leadership. The leader can of course defer to the team, and surrounding yourself with talented people is a key trait of a leader as we will see in the section on teamwork. There is, however, an expectation that the leader will constantly sharpen the saw and be at the forefront of current educational thinking. The number of leaders who are active on Twitter, constantly curating their professional development network, is testament to the importance of staying current and developing knowledge. There are also a growing number of leaders who are becoming published authors, further enhancing their expertise in the process.

 'That's excellent, that's exactly what it is – re-professionalised.'
Professor Michael Young

To hear more from **Professor Michael Young,** scan this QR code.

Modern leaders need to continue to develop themselves in order to develop others. Remaining in the classroom is an ideal way to do this. I discussed this at length with Dr Jill Berry who felt it so important that when she was headteacher she taught RE to every Year 7 class and she double staffed this to ensure consistency for the students. She felt this not only gave her the opportunity to develop relationships with the students, but also meant that she could see the impact of any initiative, pedagogical input or assessment device on the students and the staff. This gave her the knowledge, the credibility and indeed the empathy to work with her colleagues. This is just one way in which leaders can develop expertise and will be explored further on page 73. So, what are some other options for leaders looking to hone the vast range of knowledge, understanding and skills they need to lead a school today?

How can expertise be developed?

Here I'd like to return to Matthew Evans and his discussion of the differences between generic and domain-specific leadership skills. Matthew advocates that expertise is domain specific – we build knowledge and skill sets by doing very specific tasks:

'A lot of our expertise, I've come to believe, is domain specific. Which means that we develop our knowledge and skills by doing quite specific things in schools – by leading very specific things and doing particular jobs. And over time, we can develop that expertise, and we can make it more flexible, and we can maybe take those skills and use them in other areas. But the development of the skill and the knowledge, I think, comes first. And that transferability comes a bit later.' Matthew Evans

As Matthew outlines above, expertise is developed over time with predominantly first-hand experience of the domain the leader is working within.

Leaders who look to step outside their natural comfort zones can develop expertise more quickly as they will gain experience of different situations and of solving new problems. There is also a huge amount of literature available to assist rapid assimilation of expertise. If you take a current policy wave, such as curriculum, there is a huge amount of reading that a leader can do in this area; there are also training providers and experts who are easily accessible. This is one of the principal reasons for the existence of the Naylor's Natter podcast. Through having conversations with experts in the field, the listener can develop some knowledge and look further and deeper into a particular area. Matthew talks about flexibility. In our conversation I touched on the idea of leaders regularly moving positions around within a team, allowing the possibility for transferability of some skills and the development of new expertise.

The pandemic and the response to it has also shown us the value of immersion and trial and error. Through no fault of leaders, decisions have had to be made quickly and knowledge has had to be accumulated and assimilated rapidly. This is of course not the preferred option of deep knowledge, but it has shown that transferrable skills such as organisation, logistics and communication can be used across domains. Some of the twenty-first-century skills that have been denigrated by the evidence-based movement have actually proven to be essential tools in a leader's armoury at times of great change and crisis. Deep expertise imbued with powerful knowledge is vital for senior leaders to steer the direction of an organisation and develop their staff. Transferable skills, whilst not carrying the same value, have at least in the short term the ability to help leaders to steady the ship and respond and react to events. Both can be considered as expertise.

Naylor's nuggets

- Throw yourself in at the deep end: taking on new challenges will help you gain experience of handling situations and solving problems that are directly relevant to school leadership.
- Engage with books, blogs, articles and podcasts about school leadership. Make a note of your key takeaways and think about how you can start putting them into practice.
- Don't neglect the 'soft skills'. Expertise in effective organisation, logistics and communication is essential when decisions have to be made and actioned quickly.

Recommendation 5: Teamwork makes the dream work

Collaboration is essential to all successful leadership. The ability to lead yourself with all the characteristics previously outlined is rendered less useful – or even impotent – without the trust and support of a senior team, the backing of the academy trust or governors, and the collaboration of the staff.

 'The staff and the children have to be equal first, because you can't serve the children unless you're looking after the staff and developing them.' Dr Jill Berry

Having worked in many and various leadership teams over the years and spoken with innumerable school leaders on the podcast, I have picked up some qualities of effective teamwork that can be useful to recognise and understand, particularly for a leader new in post.

Smaller teams on the whole function much better

Smaller teams often work together better. This is equally true for primary and secondary schools but is particularly pertinent for large schools. The cycle of leadership teams is a study in itself; in my experience a team becomes successful and starts to gain some traction on its direction of travel. This sets in motion a chain of improvement across the organisation, which means that some people are being recognised and wish to progress. This can result in positions being created in leadership to incentivise teachers to stay in the school. In the short term this is of course positive; the teacher has been retained and staff and students are happy. The difficulties come when the responsibilities given are either at odds with or overlap significantly with a current member of the team. Where the responsibilities are rather niche or superfluous to the direction of travel of the organisation, the result can be too much time spent in meetings discussing them or a lack of focus on the core business. This can lead to disenfranchisement of the newly promoted leader or, arguably worse, to a bloated meeting schedule stuck in the thick of thin things. Where responsibilities overlap can be just as problematic. If the leaders work together for the common purpose, this can of course be hugely beneficial. However, this overlap can lead to confusion in decision-making, misunderstanding from staff and parents, and sadly ultimately to a decision around which leader to retain.

The larger a team becomes, the more confused its message. The large leadership team naturally hangs together rather tenuously. Whether we choose to recognise it or not, politics comes into play with leaders at various stages of ascension or descension. With smaller teams there are clear and measurable responsibilities and staff, students and other stakeholders know who is responsible and for what. With larger teams, the lines are blurry, the responsibilities overlapping and the possibility to get between the lines is omnipresent. This can lead to individual agendas being pushed at the expense of a strategic direction; it can result in some leaders taking the time and the ear of the headteacher at the expense of others. Meetings become languorous and laboured, decisions are slow and frustrations come to the fore. The end result of these bloated leadership teams, usually following an inspection, is the inevitable restructure. This strips the leadership team back to basics: a small, functioning team where decisions can be made coherently and collectively. It must be acknowledged that it is normal and natural for teachers to move on to different schools in order to progress in their careers. Any attempt to retain talented teachers by growing the team can backfire.

Think about the mix of your senior leadership team

'The selection of ministers is of no little importance to a prince; and they are good or not, according to the prince's prudence. The first thing one does to evaluate a ruler's prudence is to look at the men he has around him.' Niccolò Machiavelli, *The Prince*

Any selection of a senior team must follow all legislation and regulations around safer recruitment and equal opportunities. Leadership teams are best when they are diverse and representative. In personality terms, it is important for leaders to look behind the superhero leader tropes outlined on page 63 and think carefully about the assembling of a team. I am no dedicated fan of *The Avengers*, but my cursory basic knowledge of the franchise shows that the assembly of the Avengers could provide a useful metaphor for the selection of a leadership team. Each of the Avengers has different strengths and attributes that they bring to the team, thus creating a powerful force to be reckoned with. When recruiting for a leadership team, think about the skills that each potential candidate would bring to the table and how these skills would combine to cover all bases.

The first and most important person for any leader to work with is their immediate deputy. This is the person with whom they should have the closest working relationship and the leader who can step in for them and keep the organisation moving in the right direction. There is of course no one trait that can embody this deputy, but following on from podcast conversations with Neil

Reynolds I discovered the book *Consiglieri: Leading from the Shadows* by Richard Hytner (2014), which asks leaders to look at what kind of second-in-command they will need to complement and enhance their position. There have, of course, been many famous and successful double acts across all sorts of public arenas. Think Morecambe and Wise, Clough and Taylor, Blair and Brown. These leader and deputy relationships are hugely important in the leadership of any school. So, what lessons have we learned from the podcast here? Well, on air, not many! Leaders are naturally reticent to pigeonhole or discuss colleagues' personality traits and have this broadcast. Some of the best segments of the podcast are the sections that end up on the proverbial cutting room floor. Many of these 'off the mic' conversations regard the mix of a leadership team and I will summarise them in my own words here so they remain anonymous.

The relationship between a headteacher and their deputy (or deputies) can be bluntly and broadly expressed in the words of Richard Hytner from *Consiglieri* (2014): 'While the A is ultimately accountable for the enterprise, the Cs are the consiglieri who counsel, support and deliver for the A.' The leadership styles of both the A and the Cs can fluctuate and develop over time and there are extremities within the styles. When a leader works for an A, their brief is clear. This is a relatively easy role to deliver, in particular with a leader who fronts up the organisation. It can allow a natural C to flourish and make transformational changes with the security of the backing from their leader. The problem can come when the C leader, given confidence by the changes they have implemented, seeks to replace the A, which requires rather a different skill. Interestingly, the A often chooses a C as their direct successor, potentially with a view to continue their legacy or as a foil to their style. However, when a C ascends to headteacher they rarely want an aspiring A as their deputy and will actively seek to change this situation should it be something they inherit.

The rest of the team is a complex melting pot but is usually infused with the following ingredients.

Firstly, the **lifer**: the leader who has worked at the school since being an ECT and in surprisingly many cases was also a pupil at the school. They have steadfastly adhered to whatever policy wave or set of changes have flooded the school over the years. They are stoic, uncomplicated, respected and predictable. They are a natural ally to any new leader as they were there before they arrived and will be there long after the new leader has departed.

The second character is usually the **cynic**, the voice of the teachers and the superhero everyone turns to in times of difficulty. Stereotypically, this leader is approaching the end of a career and would like to get on with the job without too many new initiatives and revolutions blocking their slide into retirement.

Again, this leader is an essential part of the team and will be supportive of whichever leader is in charge. Just don't expect fulsome praise for your new Pupil Premium strategy.

The rest of the team is usually made up of keen, often younger and **ambitious assistant heads** looking to make an impression on the route to more senior leadership. When channelled into a valuable project working alongside the more experienced members of the team, these leaders are pivotal to the school's success. They are in the classroom and understand its complexities. They understand the messy nature of leadership from their whole-school role and can effectively deliver messages and implement strategy. When left alone or mismanaged, this enthusiasm can turn to restlessness and can cause issues. The flow of assistant heads through a leadership team is a natural cycle of improvement for both the team and the leader.

The last piece of the jigsaw to be aware of is the natural politics of any organisation. Ignore this at your peril and be quick to identify when and where it occurs. Points of transition are natural breakwaters for the establishment of new cultures. Where a leader or indeed a team member does not clearly identify and understand their new role, issues can occur.

The make-up of teams can make or break a leader. This is why many leaders often take their own team with them when they are appointed to a new headship or seek to bring in their own people as soon as possible.

Naylor's nuggets

- The team a headteacher has around them will either make or break their headship. Choose senior leaders carefully and build your team gradually, making changes where needed.
- When hiring leaders, follow safer recruitment practices, ensure your team is diverse and representative, and think about how their skill sets will add to the expertise of the team.
- Give each member of the SLT a specific role and set of responsibilities and communicate this clearly to the whole team.
- Identify and address any workplace politics quickly, particularly during points of transition.

Recommendation 6: Continue to teach

'My job as head of English was to help [my team] be the best they could be, to support and challenge them to reach their professional best. So, I think you need to be a very capable teacher, a good teacher [in order to be a leader]. I don't think if you are an outstanding teacher you will necessarily automatically be an outstanding leader. But I think if you're a poor teacher, your chances of succeeding in leadership actually aren't terribly great.' Dr Jill Berry

This has been a reoccurring and somewhat thorny discussion on the podcast. Do you have to be a great teacher to be a great leader? The arguments and points on both sides have value, so let's unpick and unpack these to allow some leadership lessons to emerge.

Firstly, being a good teacher is hugely time-consuming. This is why teachers tend to improve steadily in their first three years and then plateau (Kraft and Papay, 2014). To improve teaching, concentration has to be paid to knowledge development, pedagogical practice and lesson preparation. For ECTs, this will create huge cognitive load and will make leadership development difficult unless this is prioritised, as it is notably with Teach First. Controversially, the subject you teach may afford you more opportunities to engage with extra responsibilities. A non-evidence-based look at the number of PE teachers in leadership roles (usually pastoral) would suggest that either the leadership role is suited to a teacher with excellent communication and organisational skills or that the job of teaching PE allows time to develop and succeed in these roles.

The second issue is around whether good teachers should be promoted out of the classroom. This happens less in primary, where phase and senior leaders are often still attached to year groups and are teaching regularly, but it is a consideration for all schools. As you know, early in my career, I was promoted to become an advanced skills teacher. This is still the best role I have been privileged to hold because it has at its core professional development for both myself as a practitioner and for other teachers. The role allowed the development and cascading of current best practice with the time and resources required, arguably, for all teachers. When teachers feel as if the only route to development is to move out of the classroom, the profession is losing experience, skill and credibility and pupils are potentially losing out on months of progress. Staying in the classroom should not be seen as the antithesis of promotion; staying current and vibrant in your own practice should be at the core of every great leader.

Having been promoted to leadership, usually firstly as assistant head, there is a tension between delivering in the classroom and being available to support the leadership team. In this, in my opinion the most challenging of leadership positions, it can feel extremely difficult and comes with a huge workload, but it also has its benefits. The beauty of an assistant head's work is that they are the Janus of the team. They have credibility with leadership, staff and students alike, as they have their heads in the classroom. They understand what it is like to teach the majority of the timetable; they exist within policies and deal with challenging behaviour from 'those' students. They also sit around the leadership table, formulating strategy and direction and informing the next steps. The downside of their position is they often do not have the time, capacity or authority to determine that direction.

The deputy head has more of a strategic role, formulating policies, designing systems and managing staff. The best deputies, in my view, continue to teach. This is where they can see the fruits of their labours and the results of their decisions. The classroom often is the place where they perform the best, allowing students and staff to see a different side of the leader. For deputies who often lead on behaviour, it is vital to live within your own behaviour policy and system. If you cannot operate without recourse to sanctions separate to your policy, then change is needed. Perception governs reality if deputies are out of the classroom; it is too easy to exist in your perceived classroom and even your perceived school if you are making decisions from your office. This is of course not to say that deputies should teach all day, which would not be practical or effective, but they could take examination classes to show staff that everyone is helping to achieve the best for students. I would question the rationale for a non-teaching deputy.

I discussed this further on the podcast with Aziza Ajak, who is the vice principal of a school in East London. Aziza agreed it is 'critical' that senior leaders continue to teach and said that she found being in the classroom both 'grounding and humbling' and it supported her 'momentum and resilience'. She went on to explain how she initially learned to adapt to this dual role as both teacher and leader:

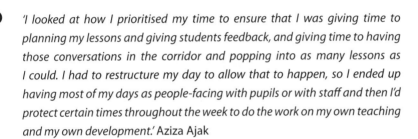

'I had to shift my mindset around my areas of responsibility. Whilst I was in charge of teaching and learning and assessment at the time, I'm fundamentally a teacher first and I love my subject. In terms of being a senior leader, my first responsibility is the safety and wellbeing of students. I had to reprioritise things in my head and accept that it was OK not to do other things to a certain standard whilst those things remained the core and the centre.' Aziza Ajak

Aziza went on to tell me how she had to adapt the structure of her day to fulfil her two roles:

'I looked at how I prioritised my time to ensure that I was giving time to planning my lessons and giving students feedback, and giving time to having those conversations in the corridor and popping into as many lessons as I could. I had to restructure my day to allow that to happen, so I ended up having most of my days as people-facing with pupils or with staff and then I'd protect certain times throughout the week to do the work on my own teaching and my own development.' Aziza Ajak

Lastly, what about headteachers? This is a section on which I bow to superior knowledge and experience, having not yet reached headship. The quote from Dr Jill Berry at the start of this section encapsulates the need for headteachers to teach. The clue is in the name 'headteacher'. Jill tells the story on the podcast of how she used to teach all Year 7 RE classes (timetabled alongside another teacher should emergencies occur) so she could get to know her pupils, see the lived reality of policies and continue to develop her own abilities as a teacher. The current models of schools are many and disparate; in academies, for example, executive headteachers and trust boards exist above the leadership of individual schools. This cushion allows breathing space for a headteacher and valuable support in areas that headteachers may not have come into the job to do, such as HR, finance and complaints. Of course, much as a football manager may not lead on every session on the training

To hear more from **Aziza Ajak**, scan this QR code.

ground, nobody expects the headteacher to deliver lessons all day. It is, however, important for staff to see the headteacher engaged in the core business of the school. A teaching headteacher remains in touch with reality and leads less by perception or by advice from their 'C' leadership colleagues. This change of perception can be hugely positive. Teaching headteachers will likely be exposed to conscientious, well-behaved and motivated students working hard. This is not always the impression given by learning walks, on-call visits and detention duties. This, in addition to what was discussed earlier, keeps the leader from the thick of thin things. The budget, complaint or HR issue will still be there after the lesson, but the joy of teaching will radiate through the leader and will be taken into their next interaction. Schools where headteachers teach should be the norm, and if not, we have to ask what is more important and what we can do to redress this.

Naylor's nuggets

- Continue to teach, whether you're a middle leader, assistant head, deputy head or even a headteacher. Most roles in school have the suffix 'teacher' and there is a reason for this. Don't lose track of your real purpose.
- When in the classroom, take note of whether the policies and procedures you have put in place are working on the ground. If not, what could be done differently?
- Keep honing your craft: no teacher is ever the finished article. There is always more to learn about the art of teaching – even for those who have reached headship.

4 Pastoral matters

Chapter overview

Pastoral care matters hugely; it always has and always will. Pastoral care has endured something of a mixed time in the education cycle over the past 20 years, but it is likely to have a huge resurgence as we continue to deal with the effects of a global pandemic and its aftermath in a society where schools have become much more than the deliverers of high-quality education. In this chapter we will examine the fall and rise of pastoral care, what good pastoral care looks like and how to create systems that value those working in this crucial area of education.

Recommendations:

Featuring podcast episodes with:

- **Stephen Lane**, May 2021
- **Professor Becky Allen**, November 2021
- **Neil Reynolds**, August 2020
- **Dave Whitaker**, May 2021

For the majority of my long career, I have been directly involved in the pastoral aspects of a school. I have vast experience as a head of year, a senior head of a learning house and as a pastoral deputy. This is the aspect of the job I've enjoyed more than any other, from the heady days as a young teacher winning the best-decorated Christmas classroom with 9F to leading 'we're all in this together' assemblies for the last ever year group of a closing school.

Whilst channel-hopping during a bout of isolation following COVID-19 illness, I happened upon an episode of the popular TV programme *Grange Hill*. This was the first episode set in the late 1970s, a time before even my experiences of school. The plot follows the first day of first-year pupils as they navigate their way to school and attempt to settle into an unfamiliar environment. Many positive changes and improvements have been made to the first-day experience since then, including transition days and summer schools, but something powerful struck me straight away. The role of the form tutor was pivotal to that first day and, in following episodes, to the entire school experience of the pupils. At Grange Hill, this form time seemed largely unstructured and relatively informal, with the tutor finding out some information about pupils and pupils about each other. There was often a visit from the omnipresent deputy head Mrs McCluskey, who never at any point asked to know what the pupils were learning or whether they were making any progress. As I followed these episodes through, the form periods were punctuated regularly by opportunities to get together as a year group for collective worship, singing and building of communities. What was noticeably absent from any of these fictionalised encounters was any discussion of interventions, catch-ups, one-to-ones and recovery reading. Times have undoubtedly changed and none more so than recently, but the importance of a teacher as the pastoral leader with a group of students seems to have diminished in favour of progress. Schools have side-lined and outsourced the pastoral care of students in favour of interventions. As a result of the fear that any pastoral time is unmeasurable and unquantifiable, every conceivable opportunity has been taken to cram in academic content. The decline of form time is just one symptom of this move away from prioritising pastoral care, which has occurred over the past decades. However, from my most recent conversations on the podcast, it is becoming evident that the COVID-19 pandemic has reminded schools of the importance of pastoral care to the life chances of pupils. Many schools are now rethinking their pastoral structure and recognising the value of time spent with pastoral staff. On an individual level, teachers will need more training on pastoral matters. In this chapter, we will consider a number of areas related to pastoral care and some key recommendations for best practice.

Recommendation 1: Avoid sacrificing form time for subject lesson time

'For me the form tutor provides an important kind of buffer between the non-school world and the school world. For some children, you know that's going to be an important sort of transition zone.'
Stephen Lane

To hear more from
Stephen Lane, scan this
QR code.

The conversation with Stephen, who is an English teacher and head of year, was particularly fascinating as it crystallised some of my thinking around the decline of form time in secondary schools. Since the controversial reign of Sir Michael Wilshaw at Ofsted, the time allotted to pastoral care has reduced significantly. This is not as a direct result of Wilshaw's or Ofsted's dictate but as a lethal mutation from statements such as this: 'As a Head, my guide was always that, if something wasn't going to impact on classroom performance then I wouldn't introduce it.' (Wilshaw, 2013)

Form time or time with a form tutor does not deliver any immediate outcomes. Its impact cannot be assessed by a flight path or a data drop, but its long-term consequences can be huge. That opportunity for connection in the morning can, as Stephen said, gently ease both the students and the teacher into the academic day ahead. It has administrative importance too, from a safeguarding perspective, through the register. Most importantly it is an opportunity for community cohesion, team building and creating a safe space. The best form teachers know their students better than other teachers. This knowledge can be vital support for the students, particularly when they maybe don't have this at home. The consistency of this time helps to prepare for the day. This is the time to rectify and support with uniform and equipment, to chase up absence and promote good attendance. This is the opportunity to develop relationships that serve the whole school community. The form tutor should be the first port of call for any issues with the student. It is difficult sometimes as a school leader to have a full picture of a year group, let alone the whole school, so the form tutor is vital in this.

The gradual erosion of form time and assemblies (which pleasingly appears to be receding) has been done under the auspices of progress. Form time has been sacrificed for intervention or catch-up, or has been cut completely to the bare minimum of administrative necessity. The result of this is of course more time with subjects, which is certainly welcome and with its own benefits. There are however knock-on effects. Centralised behaviour systems are extremely effective and provide consistency as shown in Chapter 2, but these systems sometimes do not take into account the individual circumstances of the pupils subject to them. A student who has experienced a difficult evening or morning may not be ready to learn. With proactive pastoral care, this is picked up by the form teacher. The pupil is assisted and staff are made aware. Take a pupil who has misplaced their homework as they didn't stay at home last night. Their parents call into school but are unsure who to get the message to and a detention is given. What about the pupil with a medical condition who needs a closer eye kept on them today? Or the brooding conflict between two Year 11 students, or the withdrawn Year 7 whose friends are worried about them? These are all classic pastoral issues. With the reduction in form time and the diminishment of the role of the form teacher, these are all issues that quickly become those of the classroom teacher. The subject teacher has a great deal of content to cover, knowledge to impart and work to assess. They are not unsympathetic to these issues, but due to paucity of time and resources they either don't notice the issues until they manifest as behaviour, or they pass them on through an on-call system to senior staff walking the corridors. Many schools now employ non-teaching pastoral staff who quite often are the heart of the school and will assist with any of these issues. It is my view that these pastoral issues do impact directly on classroom performance; form time is not wasted time but arguably the most important time of the day.

Form time: some tips

Here are some tips for form time done well:

- The teacher is on time and organised, greeting students personally at the door with enthusiasm.
- The tutor is the 'go to' person for their form and students feel comfortable approaching them with questions and issues.
- Form time embeds excellent routines – this consistency particularly benefits disadvantaged students.

- The students are inspected and supported to make sure they have the right equipment for the day ahead.
- Messages are delivered both individually and collectively.
- There is some unstructured time to allow for discussion and settling in.
- The form tutor creates a team ethos among the group.

Naylor's nuggets

- Form time is an essential part of the school day: it eases the transition between home and school, supports safeguarding and provides an opportunity for community cohesion and team building.
- Do not sacrifice form time for more time spent in subject lessons.
- Use form time as a way for tutors to get to know students and to:
  - provide a consistent start to the day
  - support with uniform and equipment
  - promote good attendance
  - note pastoral issues relating to individual students and resolve these or inform colleagues.

Recommendation 2: Value heads of year and other pastoral leaders

I'm pleased to say at the time of writing heads of year seem to be experiencing something of a resurgence, which in my view is welcome and required in a post-pandemic school environment. Heads of year suffered from the same mischaracterisation as form time. The job of the head of year is difficult to qualify with big data. As we know, in the early 2000s there was a policy narrative from Ofsted and school improvement partners around measuring and quantifying school improvement. The work of the head of year at that juncture was predominantly ephemeral, sorting out disagreements and dealing with issues, but the impact of a good head of year can be life changing. For school leaders, it was difficult to judge the impact of a head of year other than by perception. This bred the 'superhero' type of leaders discussed in Chapter 3 (page 63) and was not necessarily conducive to systemic change. Heads of year tended to prioritise their pastoral responsibilities (naturally) over their teaching. Speaking personally, I can vividly remember an encounter with a deputy head during my days as head of Year 7. I was having a conversation with a student (while, of course, enjoying a stone-cold brew and a Penguin) in my office, when said deputy popped his head round the door.

'Are you OK there, Sir? Need another biscuit?'

My bemused look started my thoughts racing. This level of generosity was above the normal for the deputy.

'Do you have a feeling there's somewhere you should be?'

'Erm… not that I know of.'

'Well, 30 Year 11s on the science corridor disagree!'

Cue me running down the corridor and a profuse apology to my wonderful top-set science class. This serves as an illustration of a time when this pastoral work trumped everything else in school. This did of course have its issues, not least as illustrated above for the outcomes of classes taught by the pastoral leaders. There was an understanding amongst school leaders that heads of year may not be as reliable or potentially academically effective as other colleagues, but their overall worth to the organisation was much greater and acknowledged as such. This all changed with big data. Suddenly heads of year needed to be measured, scrutinised and responsible for outcomes. The names changed too. Heads of year became progress leaders and progress managers to reflect their new responsibilities. A positive move was the supplementing and supporting of the key pastoral work with a non-teaching pastoral manager. These people, in my experience, are the heartbeat of the school and do the job from a position of care, loyalty and a genuine passion to make a difference in young people's lives. This new arrangement, on the face of it, allowed heads of year to continue teaching effectively without disruption or distraction and pastoral staff to pick up minute-by-minute developments.

Nevertheless, heads of year being responsible for academic progress, attendance and trends in behaviour made the role more problematic and arguably detached from its core purpose. The need to support students' attainment is absolutely right and the core purpose of any school. The head of year has always done this by ensuring that students adhere to the school's vision and values, behave according to expectations and are safe and well in school. Making heads of year responsible for academic progress meant huge spreadsheets and innumerable meetings. These meetings often involved heads of year asking why students were underachieving in maths or English without having any understanding of gaps in knowledge or strategies for improvement.

The 'extra set of eyes' on pupil progress may have increased pupils' motivation, but the lack of specialised knowledge meant any improvements were temporary. As head of Year 11, I conducted many revision evenings promoting transferable skills that were designed to focus students on improving exam results. It is questionable whether or not the huge volume of work was actually making a difference.

The change in inspection framework, the rise of the curriculum and the importance of knowledge transformed the role of pastoral staff again. The focus on curriculum promoted the importance of heads of department in relation to the value of knowledge in improving students' outcomes. The transferable skills promoted by 'progress leaders' were no longer recognised as effective methods to improve attainment. This rather left the progress leader in limbo as curriculum or subject leaders quickly became (rightly) responsible for the progress of students in their subjects. They, along with the teachers in their department, are best placed to address any misconceptions, plug any gaps and motivate students to achieve in their subjects.

So, what now for the progress leader and head of year? The pandemic has drawn sharply into focus the role of the school in its community. When lockdowns and partial closures hit, who was best placed to determine which students were vulnerable? Which member of staff could establish whether free school meals needed delivering? Which member of staff had the relationships with students and families to signpost them to extra support? The issue of pupils' wellbeing and mental health is the subject of other books and is beyond the expertise of the author. However, pastoral staff are often best placed to identify and signpost to specialist agencies through the depth of knowledge they have of both the students and the service providers. Schools during this time became the hub of the community as testing centres, sources of information and the location for cross-agency work. The legacy of the pandemic thus far is that pastoral care is vital to the life chances of pupils and its work is largely immeasurable by data but long lasting in its effects. The Ofsted judgement around personal development and welfare is understanding of its importance. The latest Inspection Framework states:

'The provider prepares learners for life in modern Britain by: equipping them to be responsible, respectful, active citizens who contribute positively to society; developing their understanding of fundamental British values; developing their understanding and appreciation of diversity; celebrating what we have in common and promoting respect for the different protected characteristics as defined in law.'
(Ofsted, 2019)

Nevertheless, due to the current focus on curriculum, many ambitious teachers are now less likely to move into pastoral roles due partly to their paucity and also due to the ceiling that exists in these positions. In November 2021, I spoke with Professor Becky Allen, Chief Analyst and co-founder of Teacher Tapp, the largest teacher survey in the UK, and Professor of Education at the University of Brighton. In our podcast discussion, we talked about how all 'big ideas' in education come and go. In light of this, I am convinced that the current policy wave of curriculum will recede and as Becky Allen stated on the podcast:

 'Leave beneficial sediments.' Professor Becky Allen

To hear more from
Professor Becky Allen,
scan this QR code.

These beneficial sediments may include a reassessment of the pastoral work of schools. The receding of the 'big data' wave seems to have moved the dial back to heads of year as pastoral leaders first and foremost. The move back to the ephemeral and largely unmeasurable may sound a regressive step but some of the most important work in relationships, cohesion and motivation is embodied by heads of year. Anecdotally at least, there seems to be a resurgence in interest in the role and a recognition of its importance:

 'It's the uncertainty and unpredictability which is part of the joy of it… much of what we do as pastoral leaders is reactive and ad hoc. That's what makes it so very challenging.' **Stephen Lane**

With this resurgence will come a return to career paths and opportunities for pastoral staff. If you are a teacher and have a passion for the pastoral side of the job, do not dismiss the role of head of year as your next career move. If you're a school leader, think again about how you measure the importance of your heads of year. Don't do this purely using progress measures, but consider their true impact on the lives of young people. This should also be extended to non-teaching members of staff whose opportunities for professional growth should not be stunted by their pastoral role.

Pastoral deputy heads

Like the curriculum deputy five years ago, pastoral deputies are a dying breed. Hopefully not literally, but in a landscape where curriculum dominates the work of the school, as we have seen, pastoral care can be the poor relation. The traditional pastoral deputy would have the final say on all matters related to behaviour, would oversee and line manage the heads of year and set the tone for the culture of the school through policies, procedures and routines.

Naylor's nuggets

- With the resurgence of pastoral care as we continue to deal with the effects of a global pandemic, schools will need to reassess staffing and resources. More recognition of staff choosing this area of expertise will result in sustained and sustainable care in the years to come.
- Avoid measuring the importance of pastoral staff purely in terms of progress. Think about the overall impact they have on the lives of young people.
- Make sure all pastoral staff, including non-teaching members of staff, know they have a wide range of opportunities for professional growth.

Recommendation 3: Safeguarding is everyone's business

Safeguarding is everyone's business and recent updates in the statutory guidance, 'Keeping children safe in education (KCSIE)' (Department for Education, 2021), have made this clear in both policy and expected practice. Safeguarding is also mentioned in the Ofsted Inspection Framework:

'The provider has a culture of safeguarding . . .' (Ofsted, 2019)

Safeguarding sits with all staff, but the responsibility often falls under the remit of pastoral staff. Depending on the size and context of your school, the number of referrals will vary considerably. Safeguarding is potentially an area in which teachers are more reluctant to tread. The complexities of cases, the difficult and upsetting nature of some disclosures and the overwhelming accountability can mean roles in safeguarding are difficult to recruit for and are not something that teachers aspire to.

Nevertheless, safeguarding can be hugely rewarding and the leadership of this area can be made easier with some nuggets garnered through conversations on the podcast. I have summarised some of these nuggets below.

Choose an easy reporting system

This sounds intuitive, but very often schools use complex systems that are difficult to navigate. The system must allow not only easy reporting but easy responses. A concern logged on an online system does not always mean a concern received. There are many excellent online reporting systems alongside more traditional paper-based systems. It is imperative to choose a system that suits your context best.

Make the reporting system straightforward and revisit regularly

All staff in the school should understand the reporting system and be able to articulate this clearly. Students should also know how to raise concerns with any member of staff at any time. Again, this may sound obvious but every member of staff includes cleaners, kitchen and site staff.

Make it clear who is the designated safeguarding lead

KCSIE (Department for Education, 2021) makes the responsibilities of the designated safeguarding lead (DSL) clear and has tempered this slightly by widening the responsibility to all of the leadership team. It is vital that staff know how to raise concerns and who with. It is also important to communicate what to do if the DSL is not in school and how to report concerns out of school hours. The overcommunication of these messages is vital, particularly in times of high staff absence (for example, during the COVID-19 pandemic) and during times of any school closures.

Have clarity on immediate risk of harm and the prompt reporting of incidents

As teachers we are extremely busy individuals existing in a complex and ever-changing environment. The DSL or leadership team must emphasise and constantly revisit the importance of prompt reporting. CPD alongside the statutory training must be provided and safeguarding messages must be drip-fed into staff meetings, briefings and assemblies. The sharing of positive examples via the same mediums can be useful to reinforce positive messages.

Have a triage process

In its most basic form this meeting may consist of the DSL, deputy DSL and the headteacher. This triage allows complex cases to be discussed and different perspectives to be offered. The process has transparency and scrutiny and also keeps the headteacher fully involved in what is happening in their school. In larger schools with bigger teams this may include other professionals. Confidentiality is obviously important and appropriate sharing is to be considered. Cases should be revisited, and complex cases monitored to a resolution.

Source training carefully and consider going beyond the statutory minimum

As the DSL in my school, I have ensured that all pastoral staff (heads of year, pastoral managers and SLT) have been trained to DSL level (Level 3). We have chosen an online course that contains all the updated changes to KCSIE (Department for Education, 2021) and can be completed flexibly with full concentration. Many of the online courses contain assessments which allow participants to check their understanding. Training must also be given to any new staff (including ITT and supply staff) as soon as possible and on an ongoing basis.

Work in collaboration

It is important that schools work in collaboration. This is potentially easier within academy trusts and local authorities. The overarching support and responsibility provided by external partners can be vital in understanding context, supporting local issues and providing tailored training. The opportunity to meet and discuss best practices is vital and can provide opportunities for further work and study in these areas.

Supervision is vital

In my opinion supervision is vital, particularly for DSLs. The gravity and complexity of some cases can weigh heavy on the safeguarding team. As with other professionals dealing in confidential issues (the police, health services and so on), there is no capacity to talk through these matters with loved ones or indeed some other colleagues. The triage process can help here, allowing discussion of cases and providing help and support. The job of supervision is to allow staff to unpick their thinking in a confidential environment. In my experience this is hugely beneficial, allowing an offloading and reflection opportunity, leaving the working memory of pastoral staff free to support the most vulnerable of students and staff.

Be proactive and reactive

The world of safeguarding can be fast moving, and high-profile issues and events can quickly take precedence in schools. That said, it is of course vital that the safeguarding informs the lesson planning for personal, social, health and economic (PSHE) and relationships and sex education (RSE). A well-planned, age-appropriate and coherent scheme of work for each year group is vital. In my opinion, this is most effective when it is tailored to the needs of your students, your school and your context. Within this scheme of work (as with all schemes) there should be some wriggle-room to allow for the aforementioned events to be addressed. The skills and knowledge of pastoral staff will be important for the planning here, as there will be little time to wait for resources to be developed before being delivered. The importance of addressing events as they happen can be seen by positive spikes in referrals following such lessons or assemblies. Parents are also hugely supportive of any advice that can be shared, and many schools offer information for parents through resources or by being proactive on social media. In large trusts or all-through schools, the sharing of resources and staff can be very beneficial in the delivery of RSE and PSHE.

Implementing some of the above strategies alongside the support of the school leadership team can make the work of safeguarding more amenable to aspiring leaders. The skills developed here can be extremely transferable and useful for a position on a leadership team. See the section on expertise in the leadership chapter (page 66).

Naylor's nuggets

- Safeguarding is everyone's responsibility and the culture of 'it could happen here' must permeate every educational establishment.
- Safeguarding needs resourcing, recognising and prioritising. More staff should be given training in this area and all leaders should experience the role of the DSL themselves at some point in their leadership journey.

- Teachers should spend time with the DSL to fully understand both the importance of the role and the lives of the community they serve.

Recommendation 4: Be proactive about mental health

The importance of mental health has never been greater, particularly in post-pandemic school life. Without delving into politics, services are stretched and the ability to access these for students is becoming more challenging. Schools are now looking into how best to support pupils with their mental health within the school environment. This is of course challenging, and many schools will lack the expertise and the resources to deliver this. One look at KCSIE (Department for Education, 2021) will show the direction of travel with mental health provision. All staff should be aware that mental health problems and issues can be indicators of safeguarding concerns and should be referred as appropriate and listed previously. It is important to state that only trained professionals can make diagnoses of mental health issues, but teachers are well placed to identify issues and refer and support accordingly. Some schools are moving towards a model where they have their own mental health strategy to support students and staff. Many of these are embryonic and the schools are receiving support and guidance from other agencies and professionals.

In my podcast conversation with Neil Reynolds (then the headteacher at South Shore Academy in Blackpool), we talked about his vision for an in-house mental health provision to be developed as a direct result of the continuing effects of the COVID-19 pandemic. As the discussion was 'shop talk' (we worked at the same school at the time), much of it did not make the final cut but is being shared here with Neil's permission. This is a summary and not a verbatim account.

A vision for in-house mental health provision, based on podcast conversations with Neil Reynolds

The school had identified two-to-three years ago that a significant number of students would benefit from the opportunity to see a counsellor. This was backed by the leadership of the school as a strategic pastoral priority and outsourced to an agency employing trained counsellors. It was a bold move at the time but was very much intended to support students proactively rather than potentially having to react to significant safeguarding concerns further down the line. This was successful for a period of time, thanks in no small part to the skill and expertise of the counsellor. As the pandemic hit in early 2020, we were seeing significant spikes in our safeguarding referral system and a consequent knock-on effect in counselling referrals. A member of staff working within SEND was already a trained counsellor through work done with our trust (the trust concerned employs three educational psychologists to work with SEND staff and pupils). We looked at a plan to transform an entire section of the ground floor of the school into an area to be called 'the Ark'; nominally a safe space for students to go and receive extra support for their mental health.

The plan was implemented slowly and carefully, gradually phasing the case load from one counsellor to the new in-school counsellor, whilst ensuring students were happy and comfortable with the change. A room was created to be a 'snug', which is essentially a sanctuary away from the everyday hustle and bustle of school. The snug is staffed every lesson by a qualified mental health first aider offering more informal support than the trained counsellor. A second room was commissioned to house an NHS worker who links up internal and external services, enabling a holistic, joined-up offer for students to ensure specialist care continues outside school where needed. The counsellor also links to the safeguarding team directly, working as a deputy DSL and contributing to the weekly triage as described on page 87. The counsellor sees their case load on both a formal appointment-based system and as an informal drop-in when there is an issue. Students have also been trained as mental health ambassadors and assist in the snug and Ark at break and lunchtimes. They are easily identifiable by their labelled fleece jackets and provide a vital role by being empathetic towards a student experiencing difficulties.

There is also proactive work through informing PSHE and RSE and regulating delivery in assemblies. Again, this can be planned or can be more reactionary where needed, which is often the case in a fast-moving national emergency.

Staff are supported fully through the strategy. Every member of staff is offered supervision with a trained counsellor. The leadership are offered supervision with a trust counsellor and many take this up, reporting its benefits on their mental health and pastoral practice in school. There is also rigour and scrutiny of what is delivered through regular training for all staff involved in the mental health strategy.

To hear more from **Neil Reynolds**, scan this QR code.

This provision, as eloquently explained by Neil before the podcast, is a vision into the future of mental health in schools. Wellbeing is now so much more than collapsed curriculum days, occasional assemblies and information videos. Pastoral leaders will be expected to be knowledgeable about and understanding of the importance of mental health. They will be expected to be able to refer to agencies and support students working inside school. Neil's vision and experiences are hopefully useful here to highlight how schools and leaders can take a proactive approach to the implementation of a mental health strategy.

Naylor's nuggets

- The role of schools in supporting mental health is increasing. This requires guidance, funding and training.
- School leaders can begin to be proactive about supporting the mental health of both staff and students. The impact of the pandemic means this involves much more than wellbeing; it requires a systemic change to how schools operate.

Recommendation 5: Use nurture and pathways groups for a more nuanced approach to behaviour

The topic of behaviour has been addressed in Chapter 2, page 37, but as demonstrated in all chapters in the book, behaviour has an impact on many other areas of school life. Having had the privilege of working in Blackpool for a number of years, I am a huge supporter of the work all stakeholders have done to address the root causes of the town's previously high exclusion figures. The debate around school exclusions rages on and is likely to do ad infinitum. One positive early step

Pastoral matters

taken when I started working with Dave Whitaker was to look beyond the figures at the children behind the statistics.

 'We believe every child deserves the very best care, attention, support, guidance and, dare I say it, love we can give them as caring professionals.' Dave Whitaker

Dave is the Director of Learning at a large academy trust and he has worked with us at South Shore Academy to help with a continuation of provision project for the Blackpool Opportunity Area. Dave, as discussed in depth on the podcast, helped us to identify that a high percentage of students who were classified as SEND had been either fixed-term excluded or permanently excluded nationally. Some schools in Blackpool have very high percentages of SEND students and provide tailored high-quality education for all students. The project Dave and his team were working on at this time was focused on inclusive practices, helping schools to reduce the need for, but not explicitly the numbers of, exclusions across Blackpool. For schools that were new to this project, it provided a tremendous opportunity to rethink the inclusivity of their curriculum and with that help to reduce exclusions.

In addition to this, some schools have either experimented with or set up nurture classes, predominantly for Year 7 students as a base to aid the transition from Year 6 to 7. Nurture classes are modelled on the work of Nurture UK, a charity that aims to ensure every child receives 'the support they need to have the best possible chance in life'. Reading more about the work of Nurture UK and their six principles is highly recommended. These principles are:

- *Children's learning is understood developmentally*
- *The classroom offers a safe base*
- *The importance of nurture for the development of wellbeing*
- *Language is a vital means of communication*
- *All behaviour is communication*
- *The importance of transitions in children's lives*

Source: www.nurtureuk.org/what-is-nurture

As a direct result of all of this work, some of the schools in Blackpool (those with the highest numbers of SEND students) redesigned sections of their settings to accommodate bespoke nurture groups for Key Stage 3 students and so-called pathways groups for Key Stage 4 exam groups. The nurture groups aimed to adhere broadly to the principles outlined previously, with the requisite staffing, culture and rooming. The pathways groups were a combination of the nurture principles with alternative provision and bespoke examination courses for each pupil. School leaders developed panels to meet termly to discuss transitions into and out of the group to ensure that no child fell through the cracks. The groups were staffed by classroom teachers, key workers, teaching assistants and alternative provision co-ordinators to truly provide a nurturing experience.

To hear more from **Dave Whitaker**, scan this QR code.

The conversation with Dave highlighted for me the importance of changing an approach to best fit with the children in your context. It also reinforced the importance of implementation. The schools discussed here in Blackpool went about planned systematic change to their buildings, staffing, resources, curriculum, and teaching and learning. They did not simply change their approach to 'reduce exclusions' without logically and systemically addressing the issues that potentially sit behind high exclusion figures.

Naylor's nuggets

- The use of nurture and pathways groups may support students with SEND and additional needs, especially if they are at the edge of exclusion.
- Consider a more nuanced approach to behaviour that takes into consideration the individual context of students with additional needs.

Recommendation 6: Mobile technology

'Phones are black holes for the real estate of our attention: banning them in schools is a no-brainer.' Tom Bennett (2021)

The latest iteration of KCSIE (Department for Education, 2021) has changed the pastoral landscape with regard to safe use of devices and the internet. Since the early days of mobile data and smart devices, schools have tried to stay up to date in both their usage and advice. There have certainly been times when mobile phone use has been encouraged as the future of learning, most recently during the early stages of lockdown in March 2020. Circumstances have changed somewhat and the explosion of 'content' on social media has meant that tracking pupils' use of these devices and networks has become a significant part of a pastoral leader's day. On the other side of the argument, and something discussed with Tom Bennett on his podcast about *Running the Room* (2020), there are a sizeable number of teachers and leaders who would prefer to see phone-free schools.

The benefits of technology are many and varied. However, technology use has declined somewhat in schools in an era where more traditional teaching has begun to dominate. Ten years ago, technology through phones, tablets and laptops was heralded as the next natural step for education, not to mention the omnipresent but largely pointless smartboard. Schools entered into contracts with families around the deployment of laptops in technology schemes in a bid to keep pace with developments. The laptops were often carried around by keen, enthusiastic Year 7 students for the first few weeks of term before they and the teachers realised that the process of typing, saving and sending work was much more onerous than the archaic but effective system it was designed to replace.

Fast forward to the present day and we are at a juxtaposition with technology. During lockdowns and partial closures, schools flip immediately and relatively seamlessly (in the second, third, fourth… and counting partial closures) to an entirely technology-based approach. Lessons are facilitated and augmented by technology via Teams, Google and so on. When students return to school, on the whole this technology is parked and normal service resumes.

The issue from a pastoral standpoint is not the technology itself but the social media that is attached to technology. In 2022, the phone is not a phone. Well, it is a phone, but its predominant use is not what it was designed for. The issues in school that emerge as a result of social media can become too complex and unwieldy for a school to investigate. At the time of writing, schools are reeling from a tsunami of videos uploaded to social media giant TikTok. Many of these videos are openly critical of teachers with a significant number making serious allegations linked to school names whilst masquerading as school accounts. The issue for pastoral staff is that if we allow students to bring technology into school that may supplement their learning, can we live with the unintended consequences? These can be bullying, mental health issues and potentially police investigations in the case of image sharing, for example. For a few years schools have had to walk the tightrope of risk versus reward, which has often resulted in pastoral staff becoming embroiled in complex issues that inevitably detract from their core purpose as outlined earlier in this chapter.

The current version of KCSIE (Department for Education, 2021) has almost entirely taken this out of leaders' hands, as it is not possible to allow 'safe' mobile phone usage when this is unrestricted, in a move broadly welcomed by the profession.

'Online safety and the school or college's approach to it should be reflected in the child protection policy' and this should address 'the use of mobile and smart technology', online peer-on-peer abuse and relationships on social media (Department for Education, 2021).

Leaders will now be reluctant to allow unrestricted and unvented access to 4G or 5G in school, such is the potential for safeguarding and behaviour issues. The pragmatic pastoral leader will have initiated a mobile phone 'ban' or a protocol to ensure phones are not used during the school day whilst avoiding provocative language and ensuring students can contact parents on the way to and from school. Having spoken to school leaders who have taken this step, I have heard that the response has been overwhelmingly positive from staff, students and parents.

'Students now speak to each other at break and lunchtime. Ball games have returned in the yard. Students report that they feel relieved they can escape their phone and the constant accessibility it brings. They report feeling calmer, safer and more in control. They are also honest enough to admit that they would never give up their phones but they like the fact that this choice has been taken away.' Unattributed off-air quote, September 2021

The flip side of this is the unregulated and unfettered access to mobile technology during partial closures. This is literally famine to feast and through no fault of anyone, this access is unregulated. Parents working from home are often busier, more stressed and have little time to check internet history or messages on smartphones. The partial closures have potentially damaged us all in ways that will transpire in time, but the pastoral legacy is huge. The next generation of pastoral leaders will have to understand the technology, its force for good and its dark underbelly, in the years to come.

Naylor's nuggets

- Think carefully about policies around mobile phone usage. Where do you want the pastoral team's focus? Sorting out issues from outside of school that could and arguably should be addressed by parents and other agencies?

- Do not be afraid to initiate strict protocols to ensure phones are not used during the school day. The positive changes and lack of resistance may surprise you and children may welcome the opportunity to be unconnected for a few hours.

5 What's next in education? Conversations of the future

Chapter overview

The future of education is extremely challenging to predict with any certainty, especially at such a turbulent time. However, the podcast has illuminated several core themes that are likely to influence policy and practice over the next few years. This chapter draws out these conversations and discusses the implications for teachers and school leaders.

Recommendations:

Featuring podcast episodes with:

- **Mark McCourt**, August 2019
- **Harry Hudson and Roy Blatchford**, January 2022
- **David Weston**, September 2019
- **Dr Jill Berry**, October 2019
- **Simon Cox**, January 2019
- **Professor Guy Claxton**, May 2021
- **Professor Daniel Muijs**, May 2019
- **Professor Toby Salt**, February 2022

'It's tough to make predictions, especially about the future.' Yogi Berra

This is without doubt the most difficult chapter to write. Predicting the future in education is hard enough at the best of times but during a global pandemic it is highly challenging. The only certainty is that education will continue in some form, and we are likely to see a desire, if not a need, for change. I spoke in detail with Mark McCourt on one of my favourite podcasts about the cyclical nature of education. His experience reinforced a story told earlier in the book about the idea that concepts, approaches, pedagogies and ideologies change over a 20-year period. Alongside this longer-term change, there is the type of change that occurs as a reaction to national policy, a change of leadership or the latest education trend. Factor in the preparation for and reaction to any recent change in inspection framework, or any recent or upcoming inspection, and you have all the ingredients for reactionary change.

 'Knee-jerk reactions happen all the time in education and are not helpful.' Mark McCourt

To hear more from **Mark McCourt**, scan this QR code.

With the above in mind, what are the useful remnants of both the last policy wave and the response and reaction to the ongoing pandemic? From the podcasts and some of the themes coming through the book, in this chapter I will explore the areas where recent changes are more likely to take hold, formulating policy, practice and natters into the next few years.

Recommendation 1: Teaching needs to be re-professionalised

 'In the eyes of too many people, teaching is indeed not even truly a "profession" akin to other professions. In the popular imagination, it is not on a par with medicine, law or accountancy, engineering, architecture, or business. It is not held in the same esteem as careers that are of equivalent (or indeed

less) importance to society, but to which society nonetheless gives greater kudos.'
Harry Hudson and Roy Blatchford

A back-of-a-fag-packet calculation on the number of guests whose parents or family members are or were teachers would show the statistics to be around 90 per cent. Taken positively this means that having lived, first-hand experience of the joy of teaching and its effects on people's lives makes people much keener to experience this themselves. On the other side of that argument is that teaching is seen as a safe option, an easy dynasty to be continued without huge aspiration.

To hear more from **Harry Hudson** and **Roy Blatchford**, scan this QR code.

I have interviewed some educators who fell into teaching following failed or stilted careers, some who transitioned into teaching following government campaigns or incentives, and others who worked their way through other positions in school to end up in the classroom. I have of course interviewed teachers who always aspired to be teachers from their earliest days.

'I lined up all my teddies to teach them things. I had a mini whiteboard and marker pens, and I was trying to show them how to do times tables.' David Weston

I have yet to interview any teacher who came into teaching for the pay or for the opportunity to progress through a clear structure. Still fewer have I interviewed who cited academic challenge or the opportunity to further enhance and develop knowledge of their subject.

To hear more from **David Weston**, scan this QR code.

What's next in education? Conversations of the future

99

As we look to what is next in education, from speaking with guests like Harry Hudson, it is clear that teaching needs to be re-professionalised.

Teaching is, in some people's eyes, in need of a positive rebrand to increase the awareness of its societal importance and to recruit the next generation of teachers. During lockdowns and partial school closures, parents and wider society quickly realised the innate challenges of teaching when home-schooling their own children. The complexities and demands of subjects and the required knowledge to teach them became a challenge for many, especially me. Teaching has also shown how it reaches far into the local community, connecting with local families and delivering food parcels and laptops. The diverse career paths within schools as large organisations have been illustrated through the pastoral work of teaching assistants, reception staff and wider site teams. The role of IT staff, flipping overnight to online classrooms, shows the quality and specialisation of staff within schools and trusts. As the roadmap to 'normality' stretches out in front of us, the prevailing passive-aggressive, negative narrative around teaching can be interrupted.

Now is the time to look differently at teaching. Having interviewed over 150 guests on the podcast, I am in the blessed and privileged position to look at the talent pool that exists within teaching and the myriad opportunities that exist within the field. New entrants to the profession now have a great opportunity to develop professionally without the 'sink or swim' philosophy that prevailed at the start of my career. Early career teachers now have the opportunity to develop their knowledge and practice 'on the job', supported by external providers and internal coaches. Thanks to advances in technology made explicit by lockdowns, many qualifications can be completed within and around existing school days without huge logistical operations. This re-professionalisation means that teachers should now have opportunities to progress both financially and managerially without always leaving the classroom. Many opportunities exist for teachers to work within their school or across schools via academy trusts and on a regional and national level. There are also huge opportunities to progress to jobs where salaries are in some way commensurate with what well-qualified graduates could command in the private sector. This of course needs further development but is beyond the scope or expertise of this book.

Opportunities to expand and develop teachers' knowledge are also developing, thanks to a focus on the curriculum and what Michael Young calls 'powerful knowledge'. He explains, 'It is distinct from the "common sense" knowledge we acquire through some everyday experience' (Young et al., 2014). There is an expectation and a need for teachers to understand their subject deeply and to be able to explain its key concepts. This is in direct contradiction to the narrative at the time of my training, which was that a good teacher can teach anything. The ideas of pedagogy ruled supreme over the need for knowledge. In the future, professional teachers will need the academic qualifications and professional training to ensure that they are able to deliver powerful knowledge to all pupils. As you will see in the next section, this will need to be supplemented and augmented by effective pedagogy, an understanding of how learning happens and effective technology.

As discussed in the earlier chapter on pastoral matters, there is a huge need for expertise within schools for non-teaching staff. With the shrinking of the state, many areas of health, social care and even the police are now facets of the twenty-first-century school. There are increasing opportunities for professionals within these areas to be employed by schools so they can co-exist and work across agencies to support children. These are jobs perhaps taken on as extras by teachers without the requisite training or experience. In the foreseeable future, multi-agency working within school hubs will become the norm, meeting children and families where they are and supporting communities. There are also potentially lucrative and developmental roles within trusts for accountants, HR advisors, social media experts, and marketing executives. Schools and academies in the next five to ten years will look very different from today.

Naylor's nuggets

- It is naturally difficult to make predictions, but the advancements in evidence and research may see an interruption to the cyclical nature of educational policy and practice. This will allow education to move away from ideology, fad and political influence and into the capable hands of teachers and the profession.
- The 're-professionalising' of teachers through subject knowledge enhancement, professional qualifications and grassroot movements will help to attract the best qualified graduates keen to forge a career path in public service.
- The heightened status of the profession and the commensurate pay and opportunities will ensure that recruitment and retention are less of an issue.

Recommendation 2: All teachers must teach, including the headteacher

Academisation has seen many changes to education. A tiny but significant change seems to be the naming of leadership positions within schools and trusts. Many academies now use the American terms for leaders such as principal or vice principal. 'So what?', you may say, but in my view moving forwards these subtle, nuanced semantics may lead to a change in the way schools are run.

Before I plough this particular furrow, I must declare *mea culpa*. Following many years of teaching alongside my senior leadership positions, I fell out of the classroom as schools reopened after the COVID-19 closures. I could point to tangible reasons, including the sizeable increase in the workload of senior leaders. This would however be a denigration of my key role within school. The semantics matter is best summed up by Naylor's Natter guest John Tomsett (2021): 'Be the headTEACHER, it's your core business.'

This will be vital moving forwards in education. From my exiled position, my views became nostalgic – 'I didn't do that', 'As head of department, I always…' – and ideological – 'We must do this.' Even a short slippage of time led to an isolated and outdated view of the impact of policies and procedures. Cushioned and protected within the 'vinyl suite' office, myths and legends can grow and perception can cloud reality. In an attempt to arrest this slide into dislocation, I met with our head of science. I asked him to put me back into the classroom working alongside an extremely talented ECT in what would hopefully be a mutually beneficial situation. I asked for the line management structures, instructional coaching and professional learning to apply to me in exactly the same way (as it of course should). The difference has been palpable. I now understand what it is like to work within my own behaviour policy. I have a full appreciation of the demands of assessment. I am seeking to improve my own pedagogy, subject knowledge and practice.

John Tomsett (2021) quotes in his blog: 'As Viviane Robinson points out, remaining in close touch with the classroom enables school leaders to experience first-hand (and subsequently remove because their teaching is impeded just like their teacher colleagues') the barriers preventing teachers from doing their job.' This may sound a romanticised view of the role of headteachers in a throwback to Mr Chips. Headteachers now are more like CEOs of big organisations; their days are filled with finance, HR, health and safety (currently), complaints, meetings, and policy strategy. This needs to change. The core business of any school is teaching and learning. Headteachers ascend to their leadership roles through their passion for making a difference to the lives of young people. This simply cannot be done behind the closed doors of a remote office. With the rise of academy trusts, there are arguably better qualified and certainly more specialist professionals who can deal with the logistical, financial and mechanistic facets of a school. The headteacher should be literally the 'leading learner', and this starts in the classroom.

'The fact that I continued to teach throughout my headship made a statement.'
Dr Jill Berry

Moving forwards in education, I would like to see an expectation that senior leaders remain in the classroom for a period of time. This should be rotated to allow for presence of and accessibility to leaders for staff and students. The statement being made is that we all have a common purpose and we all understand the demands of the profession. This allows senior leaders to make more empathetic and evidence-informed decisions from the vantage point of the classroom.

To hear more from **Dr Jill Berry**, scan this QR code.

Naylor's nuggets

- All teachers should teach, including the headteacher and other senior leaders.
- The core business of any school is teaching and learning. The headteacher should be the 'leading learner' and should find other more specialist professionals to deal with the logistical, financial and mechanistic facets of a school.

What's next in education? Conversations of the future

103

Recommendation 3: Education should be more evidence-informed – intrinsically

'Evidence-based leadership… helps protect schools from unsubstantiated management and teaching fads [and,] when done well, improves relational trust within schools.' Dr Gary Jones (2018)

The vast majority of our podcasts have been focused on evidence- and research-informed practice. This was our reason for existing in the first instance. It was a gamechanger for me when I became involved with the Research School movement. In the earliest conversation on the podcast, we discussed with Simon Cox about what used to drive decision-making in education:

 'If we aren't using evidence, what are we using?' **Simon Cox**

To hear more from Simon Cox, scan this QR code.

When you begin to unpick this thread, it is evident that much of the decision-making was based on ideology, instinct, hunch or tradition. That isn't intrinsically a bad thing and many great decisions and successful schools have been founded on an amalgamation of these. The issue comes when we begin looking for 'best bets' and things most likely to work.

In the early days of the latest wave of research-informed and evidence-led education, it was relatively easy to make swinging changes to prevailing norms by citing these best bets. Edu-fads and gimmicks were quickly (and rightly) swept aside by the momentum of the movement. In their place developed stock phrases added to the vernacular of school leaders: 'the evidence says', 'the evidence is clear', and many more. These in and of themselves made lethal mutations inevitable. The research and evidence movement has been a victim of its own success in that regard, with the sheer number of research studies and evidence papers making it difficult for teachers to see the wood for the trees. The EEF has of course been the voice of reason in a crowded field and has allowed teachers and school leaders to navigate the woods and establish what is best for their school in their context.

The enthusiasm around research and evidence through grassroots movements like researchED shows no signs of abatement. The two-year hiatus has potentially reinvigorated the desire for teachers to engage with each other professionally and learn from each other, which is hugely valuable. The voice given to teachers by conferences, podcasts, vlogs and publications ensures that there isn't a disconnect between the research and its application and provides clear evidence of its validity with real professionals in real classrooms. This connection is organic and vital; attempts to bring this into organised and accountable structures should be carefully considered. The petri dish environment of grassroots teacher movements allows experimentation with evidence, which is crucial to testing teachers' voracity for new ideas.

Evidence and research will be very much here to stay and helping to shape the profession for years to come in the way evidence-based medicine has done for healthcare. Its prominence and popularity may dwindle thanks to the aforementioned circuity of educational policy, but its influence will still be key. The reliance on research and evidence works in the overall re-professionalisation and rebranding of teaching. Teaching as a respected and academic profession needs the same status and mechanisms as medicine and law. Decisions on the nation's future cannot be legitimately based on ideology and hunch and left open to the political winds of change. The educational cycle may continue to turn, but it will spin with new research and the latest evidence will be implemented slowly and carefully for the betterment of all.

Naylor's nuggets

- Evidence and research will remain influential in education for years to come and will help teaching to build its status as a respected and academic profession.
- Teachers must continue to engage with and learn from one another through conferences, podcasts, vlogs and publications. This helps to bridge the gap between research and its application in the classroom.

What's next in education? Conversations of the future

105

Recommendation 4: Let's meet in the middle

'The road to educational hell is paved with false dichotomies.' Sir Michael Barber (quoted in Claxton, 2021)

One of my favourite and most-listened-to episodes featured the effervescent Professor Guy Claxton, a passionate cognitive scientist and author of many visionary books on the process of learning. The reason for the popularity of this episode and its position in my 'favourite' interviews is that, for me, it meets teachers where they are and sets out a claim for the middle ground in education.

Anecdotally, most teachers do not engage with teacher social media. An interesting side note here is that the majority of teachers in my school are unaware of Naylor's Natter, despite working in the same building as me. This is not a criticism and indeed working with me may preclude teachers from wanting to hear any more from me. This does serve as an example of perception versus reality in the world of education. The large majority of teachers in school do not engage in education debates on Twitter, Instagram or Facebook. However, many more teachers than ever before are engaged in their own professional development through books, podcasts, vlogs and blogs. This interesting praxis in education results in the majority of teachers delivering learning with a pragmatic approach. Lessons will contain the best elements of knowledge and skills, along with combined wisdom and practice of the department, phase or school.

Doing the podcast for four years has allowed me to straddle the educational divides, to pick up ideas, knowledge and wisdom from both sides of the table. To quote Jo Cox (2015) (out of context), I have found: 'We are far more united and have far more in common with each other than things that divide us.'

The middle ground in any genre or walk of life is hardly likely to inspire devotion, fanaticism or a huge amount of interest but it is likely to be popular and widely trodden. Listeners to the Vinyl Suite section of the podcast (see page 5) will have heard many left-field choices from guests seeking to display their renaissance and somewhat niche tastes. Some guests, including the wonderful Dave McPartlin, have been happy to plough the furrow for middle-of-the-road artists such as Dire Straits, rather than Simon Cox's William Basinski loops. This analogy is useful, as the false dichotomies often played out on social media are not in many people's experience the status quo in staffrooms up and down the country. Many teachers and indeed school leaders may not be aware of certain educational camps or be driven by ideology. They simply want what is best for their students, staff and community in their context. The importance of knowledge and the re-professionalising of teachers are crucial for the next steps in education, but as Guy Claxton (2021) states: 'There is no one best way to teach. There are no unqualified answers to "What works?". You have to specify your values, goals, aims and intentions. How you teach depends on what you are teaching for.'

This is profoundly important for what's next in education. As Guy asserts in his book, there is little evidence that progressive 'nonsense' is rife in schools. Aside from the fabled deconstruction and renunciation of 'learning styles' and 'Brain Gym®', there is little that is universally deployed and even less that is used contrary to evidence and research. Teachers, now re-professionalised, will have an understanding of what the future is going to hold for their students. They will be able to combine knowledge with skills and habits within a curriculum that takes into account experiences and engagement. Instructional coaching and professional development have seen a refocusing on pedagogy underpinned by strong subject knowledge. The need to present the knowledge in a way that stimulates and engages learners is, and will continue to be, important. Creating a culture and a climate of good behaviour and positive relationships will enable and enhance good outcomes for all learners.

Education will in my view move towards a centre ground, meeting real teachers where they are. As being evidence-informed becomes systemic and systematised and nostalgia, ideology and political pressure recede, teachers and leaders will be better informed to make their own decisions based on what is most likely to work for them in their context, guided by the cumulative expertise of the profession.

To hear more from **Professor Guy Claxton**, scan this QR code.

Naylor's nuggets

- There is no best way overall to teach according to more learned minds than mine. Let's take the best that has been thought, said and written and apply it to our learners in our classrooms in our context.
- The profession can retain the intellectual curiosity and the ability to challenge each other without the propagation of false dichotomies.

What's next in education? Conversations of the future

107

Recommendation 5: Implementation matters and takes time

As a profession we need to move away from guesswork and grasping for solutions before we have identified the problems we would like these solutions to fix. Physician Martin Fischer (1879–1962) said that 'diagnosis is not the end, but the beginning of practice' (quoted in Didau, 2015). In terms of school improvement plans and target-setting, it is timely to look at how school leaders identify and select priorities for their schools. Too often the approach to this appears to resemble '. . . a doctor trying to treat a patient's condition without an accurate thermometer and with little knowledge of medical research' (AEE, 2017). This is hardly surprising, particularly for schools and leadership teams in challenging circumstances where the pressure to deliver quick remedies and sticking-plaster treatments is prescient.

So how do leaders set about diagnosis in these circumstances? Quite often, due to the national or regional landscape, the agreed narrative is the starting point. A pressurised leadership team in an Ofsted category looking to move quickly naturally grabs hold of ideological solutions to these nationally recognised problems. They look to the school down the road that marks the books of Pupil Premium students first; the school the deputy came from which takes their underachieving students bowling; or the academy chain's flagship school in a leafy suburb which has introduced Saturday mastery classes for high-attainers.

A lack of diagnosis leads to guess work, solutions looking for problems, and leaves the school with an initiative and intervention overload. This approach can drain our teachers, confuse our parents, and distract our students.

William Edwards Deming (1900–1993), an American engineer, statistician and professor, said that 'without data, you are just another person with an opinion' (quoted in Didau, 2015). Leadership teams using data from examinations and assessments is clearly better than blindly following the nationally agreed narrative; measuring the symptoms of the condition allows for more accurate diagnosis.

Data is important, but leaders must be careful not to attribute correlation with causation. Quite often, to extend our medical analogy, by the time the symptoms appear it may be too late to treat the cause: the primary school with low phonics scores for its Pupil Premium students due an inspection at the end of Year 1 launches into a one-to-one reading programme. Its data shows a 33 per cent improvement so it scales up for the following year – but the 33 per cent was down to one pupil who had missed five sessions due to dentist treatments.

The data must be part of a root and branch audit of the school's current practice. An example would be the Teacher Development Trust's audit process for CPD, which looks at culture, focus, needs analysis and, crucially, research, innovation and evidence, carefully building CPD programmes to support this need.

This audit will identify themes for schools in their context. For example, many schools in the government's 'opportunity areas' have identified that the literacy levels of students are the main conditions causing the symptoms of low attainment, poor engagement and a widening of the Pupil Premium gap. The data may show that reading scores are low but a full audit including all stakeholders may reveal that decoding is good, but comprehension is poor, thereby allowing schools to define a very tight area of focus.

A positive by-product of this approach is the stripping away of many interventions that do not directly contribute to the area of focus (is there any benefit to a trip to a water park at the weekend for the Pupil Premium students who struggle to read?). This can save money and time, and allow teachers and students to focus on evidence-based 'best bets' for these tight areas of focus. These best bets must be, in my opinion, taken from the comprehensive sets of guidance reports and toolkit suggestions from the Education Endowment Foundation (EEF).

Thomas Edison said that 'vision without implementation is hallucination' (quoted in Didau, 2015). Having specified a tight area of focus, it is important to make changes, but these need to be considered, incremental and implemented fully. The patient recovering from a heart attack needs more exercise, a healthier diet, and regular check-ups. She also needs to know that the treatments prescribed are most likely to work for her in her situation. The need for exercise is clear, but attempting to run the London Marathon the same year would be a bridge too far.

Yet how many times do we see schools identify an issue (hopefully consult some research and look for evidence-based solutions) and throw the proverbial kitchen sink of interventions at the problem – and then measure the outcomes only in the summer?

We need to take time to potentially change the curriculum, build CPD programmes and factor in full implementation with intelligent adaptation thrown in. The placebo pill of interventions might make things feel better but ultimately the issue will return if we do not go about this properly.

- Be careful of solutions looking for problems. The next shiny thing is not always needed in your context.
- Allow time for decision-making and implementation. Improvement is never instantaneous, nor should it be expected to be. Slow, steady, incremental marginal gains are important and make the longer-lasting impacts.

Recommendation 6: Tame the technological beast

'How to use technology so that you rule it rather than it ruling you.'
Professor Toby Salt

The irreversible march of technology is worth holding back before it is too late. I am a huge fan of technology. To the cost of any savings and at the expense of any financial acumen, I have always had to have the latest technology. From pagers to PalmPilots, BlackBerry® smartphones to Apple TV, I have always sought to supplement my teaching with the latest advances. The key word in the above sentence, for me at least, is 'supplement'. From my earliest days of teaching when I purchased an eye-wateringly expensive Dell laptop to save all my class spreadsheets on (to the awe and wonder of Class 9F) and a PalmPilot to schedule my (non-existent) meetings, I have tried to save time, effort and energy by using technology. Most recently, in 2019, this involved the purchase of Apple TV and an iPad to ensure I was always facing my Year 11 class, just in case!

Education during lockdowns and partial closures due to COVID-19 was enabled by technology. Much of what developed was due to the incredible advances that had lain dormant on our computers, such as conference facilities and interactive classrooms. However, many disadvantaged communities were left further disadvantaged due to the inequalities in technology and the consequent lack of access. This section does not seek to discuss the 'catch-up' agenda but looks to guard against the technological encroachment into education and the working lives of teachers. During the COVID-19 pandemic, '81% of teachers responding to [a NASUWT] survey report they have experienced an increase in workplace stress over the past year and almost half

(48%) said the job had affected their physical health' (NASUWT, 2021). It would be a stretch and an inaccuracy to extrapolate the above findings to teachers' use of technology. If we consider, however, that the average teacher has spent a significant proportion of the past year working from home, it may be possible to infer correlation if not causation.

The use of technology to supplement teaching is of course welcomed as a labour-saving and learning-enhancing measure. Visualisers, laptops and office products are long-serving and essential parts of a teacher's armoury. Office conferencing facilities such as Teams and Zoom have been a huge logistical saving device, enabling training sessions, conferences and cross-school working. The technological beast has saved countless hours of travel and expenses on petrol and has allowed much more to be accomplished on any given day. The health and safety of pupils and teachers should also be paramount, but I do not wish to discuss the politics of public health measures, as this is not my area of expertise.

 'Remote education is a means, not an end... Remote education is not the same as digital education.' Professor Daniel Muijs

Daniel Muijs is of course right here in his assertion that remote education is a useful tool, but there is a danger that when you only have a hammer you see everything as a nail. The interactivity and human connection are lost through staff briefings on Teams. The benefits of a facilitator's delivery are lost staring down the barrel of a Zoom call. Parents' evenings are doubtless more efficient via hosting software, but there is something magical about accompanying your child to their school to become wedged in a Year 3 chair. The balance of efficiency versus purpose must be carefully weighted by school leaders and their communities.

To hear more from **Professor Daniel Muijs,** scan this QR code.

The tentacles of the technological beast are far reaching. Students who spent inordinate amounts of time on devices during lockdowns have, in my experience, welcomed the return to school and the freedom to escape the online world. Many schools have instigated mobile phone policies to address the new

What's next in education? Conversations of the future

111

guidance in KCSIE (Department for Education, 2021) and to protect their students from harmful content. The beneficial by-product of this seems to be a newfound freedom to interact, play and enjoy the company of their peers. The reach as far as teachers and school staff go is the pernicious tentacle of email. The power of an email to derail or even ruin a teacher's evening or weekend should not be underestimated.

'As a leader the timing of your emails will be sending a message you may not even be aware of. To you, an email pinged at 10pm with a reminder that you want a catch up the next day is just a way of making sure you don't forget to do something. To an employee, a 10pm email from the CEO may be interpreted as a sure sign they are about to be fired, meaning they will worry sick all night. Setting boundaries is therefore good.' Professor Toby Salt (2021)

To hear more from **Professor Toby Salt**, scan this QR code.

When we spoke on the podcast, Toby and I disagreed somewhat on our views of and use of emails. I could, and still can, see his point entirely that teachers should be allowed to work as and when they need to. The idea of an email curfew (of which I am a fan) may disadvantage staff working flexibly or even new parents. The issue I have with the reach of the technological beast is that it has the potential to derail you emotionally at any time and in any situation. Thanks to my aforementioned technological predisposition, I have the latest mobile phone resplendent with many 'productivity' apps. These apps allow me to access my calendar, email, messages and calls at any time from anywhere. This was particularly useful in the periods of partial closure when, like others, every device in the Naylor household was in use and serving a function as a mobile classroom for Child 1 and 2. Since our return to school, I have engaged in a 'digital detox', to use Toby's words. This has involved migrating all work-related apps and calls to a specific work phone. This has included, somewhat surprisingly perhaps, Twitter and other social networking apps. I have withdrawn myself from work-based WhatsApp groups and have brought in an email protocol at school which I discussed with Ross McGill (@TeacherToolkit) in an article I wrote for him in 2018.

In the article, I set out a list of questions that you should consider before sending an email:

- Do I really need to send this email? How many conversations start with 'Did you get my email?'
- Do I have to send it now?
- Can I solve this issue by waiting and asking the person face to face?
- Does every single member of staff need to read it?

Some schools have adopted an email window, for example:

- No emails should be sent between the hours of 7pm and 7am from Monday to Thursday.
- No emails should be sent after 5pm on a Friday.
- This email window could apply in term time and during holiday periods.

But what about if you want to work outside this window? The good news is that it's still possible to work on emails outside of this window for teachers who wish to do so and for whom this fits better with their working lives. Teachers should always consider the 'before sending an email' questions above first.

- Write out the email, store it in your drafts and then send it in the morning.
- Alternatively, most email providers have a 'Delay Send' facility. This allows you to schedule emails days in advance.

The ability of technology to allow work to reach you wherever you are has been and will continue to be a vital part of education moving forwards. In the next few years, I hope that education can capitalise and utilise these benefits across flexible working, professional learning and multi-agency working. I would like to see teachers incorporating a digital detox and allowing themselves to 'smell the roses' occasionally. It is palpable the number of books written by leaders who wish they could be transported back to their early days in leadership and invest more in the formative years of their own children and families. These same leaders identify that the value of presenteeism is overstated. The hard yards or the extra mile may be beneficial in the short term, but the only place a leader is indispensable is in their own home. The breakneck pace of education (magnified by the rise of technology) has, in Naylor's Natter guest Stephen Tierney's (2020) words, 'Led to a manic style of leadership. What the school required was a less frenetic leader and a more phronetic one.'

The 'always on' culture of leadership with technology has meant instant and constant availability for teachers and leaders. Staff email addresses are a vital contact point for parents but have now become channels for demands, questions and sometimes complaints. The mobile phone numbers of leaders garnered at the outset of lockdown have allowed sometimes trivial and occasionally serious concerns to simply be texted to leaders for an immediate response. Comparing this with the experiences of friends working in the private sector elicits amazement that anyone who is not within working hours would even think of contacting staff. The holidays have of course never fully been such a thing. Many teachers spend significant amounts of time either catching up or preparing for the next term. Again, the technological beast has devoured the holidays, particularly for leaders. The offer of contact from external agencies, so welcomed during the pandemic, has rolled into an expectation with many meetings now scheduled during half terms and summer holidays.

Hopefully what is next in education is a pragmatic and phronetic approach to technology. Technology to save time, to aid learning and to support staff's wellbeing. Teachers and leaders require headspace to think and to be. Teachers' pedagogy and practice will benefit from a renaissance approach to living, experiencing life and sharing this to shape and form young minds. We need to tame the technological beast before it rules us.

Naylor's nuggets

- Tame the technological beast by making technology work for teachers and the profession. Enjoy its benefits through flexible working and remote access.
- Ensure that the tentacles of the beast do not pervade family and personal time. Do not get to the end of a career wishing you had been present for that birthday, watched that nativity or even attended that medical appointment.
- Be present, and model this for colleagues and young people.

Conclusion

I have decided to end the book on something of a bombshell. After almost four years and over 150 episodes, I have decided to hang up the microphone. The process of pulling together, transcribing and collectivising all the discussions from across the years convinced me that the timing is right to end our natters. We have come full circle. The vision for the podcast at the start was to showcase and highlight the work of the fabulous educational community. A chance to 'just talk to teachers' and develop myself and others professionally. Through the careful selection and combination of the work of others with my own reflections in this book, I have been able to present the best that has been thought and said on the podcast as a living resource.

The book and the back catalogue will now hopefully provide a holistic guide, a compendium of some of the best educational thinking of this fascinating time in education and our world. The interactive nature of the interviews, nuggets and podcast links will mean this book can be used for education, reflection, staffroom discussion or even a book club focus. The 18-month writing process will be worth it entirely if just one school uses this as a template for a professional learning discussion.

I stood on the shoulders of giants when taking my first tentative steps into podcasting. The legendary Craig Barton literally and metaphorically guided me through how to channel the educational talent of the teaching world. The baton can now be passed on to the many and varied educational voices hosting podcasts and I can return to being a passive observer and consumer of the audio learning available.

I still hope to platform the voices of others and to continue to learn from the vast untapped resources of the best profession in the world.

So, we are done! Four years and a book and I say farewell but not goodbye hopefully. Thank you for everyone's support with the podcast during this time. I hope the legacy of the podcast continues to support teachers over the next few years and this resource is used in schools and beyond.

References

AEE (2017), 'School interventions that work: Targeted support for low-performing students', https://all4ed.org/publication/schoolinterventions

Arnold, M. (1869), *Culture and Anarchy: An Essay in Political and Social Criticism*.

Bennett, T. (2020), *Running the Room: The Teacher's Guide to Behaviour*. Woodbridge: John Catt.

Bennett, T. (2021), 'Phones are black holes for the real estate of our attention. Banning them in schools is a no-brainer', *Telegraph*, www.telegraph.co.uk/news/2021/06/16/phones-black-holes-real-estate-attention-banning-schools-no

Canter, L. (2009), *Assertive Discipline: Positive Behaviour Management for Today's Classroom* (4th edn). Bloomington, IN: Solution Tree Press.

Claxton, G. (2021), *The Future of Teaching: And the Myths That Hold It Back*. Abingdon: Routledge.

Covey, S. (2020), *The 7 Habits of Highly Effective People* (30th anniversary edn). London: Simon & Schuster.

Cox, J. (2015), 'We are far more united than the things that divide us', Commons Address, 3rd June, London.

Dennison, P. E. and Dennison, G. E. (1989), *Brain Gym: Teacher's Edition* (revised edn). Edu Kinesthetics.

Department for Education (2021), 'Keeping children safe in education (KCSIE) 2021', www.gov.uk/government/publications/keeping-children-safe-in-education--2

Didau, D. (2015), *What If Everything You Knew About Education Was Wrong?* Carmarthen: Crown House.

Dix, P. (2017), *When the Adults Change, Everything Changes: Seismic Shifts in School Behaviour*. Carmarthen: Crown House.

Dix, P. (2021), *After the Adults Change: Achievable Behaviour Nirvana*. Carmarthen: Crown House.

EEF (2019a), 'Putting evidence to work – a school's guide to implementation', https://educationendowmentfoundation.org.uk/education-evidence/guidance-reports/implementation

EEF (2019b), 'Improving behaviour in schools: Guidance report', https://educationendowmentfoundation.org.uk/education-evidence/guidance-reports/behaviour

Ellis, S. and Tod, J. (2018), *Behaviour for Learning: Promoting Positive Relationships in the Classroom* (2nd edn). Abingdon: Routledge.

Hudson, H. and Blatchford, R. (2022), *Must Do Better: How to Improve the Image of Teaching and Why it Matters*. Woodbridge: John Catt.

Hytner, R. (2014), *Consiglieri: Leading from the Shadows*. London: Profile Books.

Jensen, E. (2008), *Super Teaching* (4th edn). London: Corwin.

Jones, G. (2018), *Evidence-Based School Leadership and Management: A Practical Guide*. London: Sage.

Kraft, M. A. and Papay, J. P. (2014), 'Can professional environments in schools promote teacher development? Explaining heterogeneity in returns to teaching experience', *Educational Effectiveness and Policy Analysis*, 36, (4), 476–500.

Lemov, D. (2021), *Teach Like a Champion 3.0: Techniques That Put Students on the Path to College*. Hoboken, NJ: Jossey-Bass.

Myatt, M. (2020), *Back on Track: Fewer Things, Greater Depth*. Woodbridge: John Catt.

NASUWT (2021), 'Covid impacts on teacher mental health exposed', www.nasuwt.org.uk/article-listing/covid-impacts-on-teacher-mental-health-exposed.html

Naylor, P. (2018), 'Email protocol for schools', *Teacher Toolkit*, www.teachertoolkit.co.uk/2018/11/12/email-protocol-for-schools

Nurture UK, 'What is nurture?', www.nurtureuk.org/what-is-nurture

Ofsted (2019), 'Education inspection framework', https://www.gov.uk/government/publications/education-inspection-framework/education-inspection-framework

Salt, T. and McInerney, L. (2021), *The Juggling Act: How to Juggle Leadership and Life*. Woodbridge: John Catt.

Teacher Development Trust, 'CPD diagnostic tool', https://tdtrust.org/cpd-diagnostic-review

Tierney, S. (2020), *Educating with Purpose: The Heart of What Matters*. Woodbridge: John Catt.

Tomsett, J. (2015), 'This much I know about... how appraisal can help improve the quality of teaching in schools', https://johntomsett.com/2015/10/11/this-much-i-know-abouthow-appraisal-can-help-improve-the-quality-of-teaching-in-schools

Tomsett, J. (2021), 'This much I know about… my old hobby-horse (all SLT should teach!)', https://johntomsett.com/2021/06/27/this-much-i-know-about-my-old-hobby-horse-all-slt-should-teach

Tomsett, J. and Uttley, J. (2020), *Putting Staff First: A Blueprint for Revitalising our Schools*. Woodbridge: John Catt.

Weston, D. and Clay, B. (2018), *Unleashing Great Teaching: The Secrets to the Most Effective Teacher Development*. Abingdon: Routledge.

Wilshaw, M. (2013), 'Raising pupil attainment', Westminster Education Forum Keynote Seminar: Raising Pupil Attainment, 7th November, London.

Young, M., Lambert, D., Roberts, C. and Roberts, M. (2014), *Knowledge and the Future School: Curriculum and Social Justice*. London: Bloomsbury.

Index